A NEW BIRTH

J.C. Ryle

BAKER BOOK HOUSE
Grand Rapids, Michigan

Reprinted 1977 by
Baker Book House

ISBN: 0-8010-7658-7

PHOTOLITHOPRINTED BY CUSHING - MALLOY, INC.
ANN ARBOR, MICHIGAN, UNITED STATES OF AMERICA
1977

CONTENTS

The Cross

GALATIANS VI. 14

"God forbid that I should glory, save in the cross of our Lord Jesus Christ."

READER,

What do you think and feel about the Cross of Christ? You live in a Christian land. You probably attend the worship of a Christian Church. You have perhaps been baptized in the name of Christ. You profess and call yourself a Christian. All this is well. It is more than can be said of millions in the world. But all this is no answer to my question, *"What do you think and feel about the Cross of Christ?"*

I want to tell you what the greatest Christian that ever lived thought of the Cross of Christ. He has written down his opinion. He has given his judgment in words that cannot be mistaken. The man I mean is the apostle Paul. The place where you will find his opinion, is in the letter which the Holy Ghost inspired him to write to the Galatians. And the words in which his judgment is set down are these, "God forbid that I should glory, save in the cross of our Lord Jesus Christ."

Now what did Paul mean by saying this? He meant to declare strongly, that he trusted in nothing but Jesus Christ crucified, for the pardon of his sins and the salvation of his soul. Let others, if they would, look elsewhere for salvation: let others, if they were so disposed, trust in other things for pardon and peace. For his part the apostle determined to rest on nothing, lean on nothing, build his hope on nothing, place confidence in nothing, glory in nothing, except the "Cross of Jesus Christ."

Reader, let me talk to you about this subject. Believe me it is one of the deepest importance. This is no mere question of controversy. This is not one of those points on which men may agree to differ, and feel that differences will not shut them out of heaven. A man must be right on this subject, or he is lost for ever. Heaven or hell, happiness or misery, life or death, blessing or cursing in the last day,—all hinges on the answer to this question, "What do you think about the Cross of Christ?"

I. Let me show you what the apostle Paul did not glory in.

II. Let me explain to you what he did glory in.

III. Let me show you why all Christians should think and feel about the Cross like Paul.

I. *What did the apostle Paul not glory in?*

There are many things that Paul might have gloried in, if he had thought as some do in this day. If ever there was one on earth who had something to boast of in himself, that man was the great apostle of the Gentiles. Now if he did not dare to glory, who shall?

He never gloried *in his national privileges.* He was a Jew by birth, and as he tells us himself,—" An Hebrew of the Hebrews." He might have said, like many of his brethren, "I have Abraham for my fore-father. I am not a dark unenlightened heathen, I am one of the favoured people of God. I have been admitted into covenant with God by circumcision, I am a far better man that the ignorant Gentiles." But he never said so. He never gloried in anything of this kind. Never for one moment!

He never gloried *in his own works.* None ever worked so hard for God as he did. He was more abundant in labours than any of the Apostles. No living man ever preached so much, travelled so much, and endured so many hardships for Christ's cause. None ever converted so many souls, did so much good to the world, and made himself so useful to mankind. No father of the early Church, no reformer, no puritan, no missionary, no minister, no layman,—no one man could ever be named, who did so many good works as the apostle Paul. But did he ever glory in them, as if they were in the least meritorious, and could save his soul? Never! never for one moment!

He never gloried *in his knowledge*. He was a man of great gifts naturally, and after he was converted the Holy Spirit gave him greater gifts still. He was a mighty preacher, and a mighty speaker, and a mighty writer. He was as great with his pen as he was with his tongue. He could reason equally well with Jews and Gentiles. He could argue with infidels at Corinth, or Pharisees at Jerusalem, or self-righteous people in Galatia. He knew many deep things. He had been in the third heaven, and heard unspeakable words. He had received the spirit of prophecy, and could foretell things yet to come. But did he ever glory in his knowledge, as if it could justify him before God? Never! never! never for one moment!

He never gloried *in his graces*. If ever there was one who abounded in graces, that man was Paul. He was full of love. How tenderly and affectionately he used to write! He could feel for souls like a mother or a nurse feeling for her child. He was a bold man. He cared not whom he opposed when truth was at stake. He cared not what risks he ran when souls were to be won. He was a self-denying man, —in hunger and thirst often, in cold and nakedness, in watchings and fastings. He was a humble man. He thought himself less than the least of all saints, and the chief of sinners. He was a prayerful man. See how it comes out at the beginning of all his Epistles. He was a thankful man. His thanksgivings and his prayers walked side by side. But he never gloried in all this, never valued himself on it, never rested his soul's hopes on it. Oh, no! never for a moment!

He never gloried *in his Churchmanship.* If ever there was a good Churchman, that man was Paul. He was himself a chosen apostle. He was a founder of Churches, and an ordainer of ministers. Timothy and Titus, and many elders, received their first commission from his hands. He was the beginner of services and sacraments in many a dark place. Many an one did he baptize. Many an one did he receive to the Lord's table. Many a meeting for prayer, and praise, and preaching, did he begin and carry on. He was the setter up of discipline in many a young church. Whatever ordinances and rules and ceremonies were observed in them, were first recommended by him. But did he ever glory in his office and Church standing? Does he ever speak as if his Churchmanship would save him, justify him, put

away his sins, and make him acceptable before God?
Oh, no, never! never for a moment!

And now, reader, mark what I say. If the apostle
Paul never gloried in any of these things, who in all
the world, from one end to the other, who has any
right to glory in them in our day? If Paul said,
God forbid that I should glory in anything whatever
except the cross, who shall dare to say, "I have something to glory of,—I am a better man than Paul?"

Who is there among the readers of this book that
trusts in any goodness of his own? Who is there
that is resting on his own amendments, his own morality, his own performances of any kind whatever?
Who is there that is leaning the weight of his soul
on anything whatever of his own in the smallest
possible degree? Learn, I say, that you are very
unlike the apostle Paul. Learn that your religion
is *not apostolical religion*.

Who is there among the readers of this book that
trusts in his Churchmanship, for salvation? Who is
there that is valuing himself on his baptism, or his
attendance at the Lord's table,—his church-going on
Sundays, or his daily services during the week,—and
saying to himself, What lack I yet? Learn, I say,
this day, that you are very unlike Paul. Your
Christianity is *not the Christianity of the New Testament*. Paul would not glory in anything but the
Cross. Neither ought you.

Oh, reader, beware of self-righteousness! Open sin kills its thousands of souls. Self-righteousness kills its tens of thousands. Go and study humility with the great apostle of the Gentiles. Go and sit with Paul at the foot of the cross. Give up your secret pride. Cast away your vain ideas of your own goodness. Be thankful if you have grace, but never glory in it for a moment. Work for God and Christ with heart and soul and mind and strength, but never dream for a second of placing confidence in any work of your own.

Think, you who take comfort in some fancied ideas of your own goodness,—think, you who wrap up yourselves in the notion, "all must be right, if I keep to my Church,"—think for a moment what a sandy foundation you are building upon! Think for a moment how miserably defective your hopes and pleas will look in the hour of death, and in the day of judgment! Whatever men may say of their own goodness while they are strong and healthy, they will find but little to say of it when they are sick and dying. Whatever merit they may see in their own works here in this world, they will discover none in them when they stand before the bar of Christ. The light of that great day of assize will make a wonderful difference in the appearance of all their doings. It will strip off the tinsel, shrivel up the complexion, expose the rottenness, of many a

deed that is now called good. Their wheat will
prove nothing but chaff. Their gold will be found
nothing but dross. Millions of so-called Christian
actions will turn out to have been utterly defective
and graceless. They passed current, and were valued
among men. They will prove light and worthless
in the balance of God. They will be found to have
been like the whitened sepulchres of old,—fair and
beautiful without, but full of corruption within.
Alas! for the man who can look forward to the day
of judgment, and lean his soul in the smallest degree
on anything of his own!*

Reader, once more I say, beware of self-righteousness in every possible shape and form. Some people
get as much harm from their fancied virtues as others
do from their sins. Take heed, lest you be one. Rest
not, rest not till your heart beats in tune with St.

* "Howsoever men when they sit at ease, do vainly tickle
their own hearts with the wanton conceit of I know not what
proportionable correspondence between their merits and their
rewards, which in the trance of their high speculations, they
dream that God hath measured and laid up as it were in
bundles for them ;—we see notwithstanding, by daily experience, in a number even of them, that when the hour of death
approacheth, when they secretly hear themselves summoned
to appear and stand at the bar of that Judge, whose bright-
ness causeth the eyes of angels themselves to dazzle, all those
idle imaginations do then begin to hide their faces. To name
merits then is to lay their souls upon the rack. The memory
of their own deeds is loathsome unto them. They forsake all
things wherein they have put any trust and confidence. No
staff to lean upon, no rest, no ease, no comfort then, but only
in Christ Jesus."—*Richard Hooker.* 1585.

Paul's. Rest not till you can say with him, "God forbid that I should glory in anything but the cross."

II. Let me explain, in the second place, *what you are to understand by the Cross of Christ.*

The cross is an expression that is used in more than one meaning in the Bible. What did St. Paul mean when he said, "I glory in the cross of Christ," in the Epistle to the Galatians? This is the point I now wish to make clear.

The cross sometimes means that wooden cross on which the Lord Jesus was nailed and put to death on Mount Calvary. This is what St. Paul had in his mind's eye when he told the Philippians that Christ "became obedient unto death, even the death of the cross." (Phil. ii. 8.) This is not the cross in which St. Paul gloried. He would have shrunk with horror from the idea of glorying in a mere piece of wood. I have no doubt he would have denounced the Roman Catholic adoration of the crucifix, as profane, blasphemous, and idolatrous.

The cross sometimes means the afflictions and trials which believers in Christ have to go through if they follow Christ faithfully, for their religion's sake. This is the sense in which our Lord uses the word, when He says, "He that taketh not his cross, and followeth after Me, cannot be my disciple." (Matt. x. 38.) This also is not the sense in which

Paul uses the word, when he writes to the Galatians. He knew that cross well. He carried it patiently. But he is not speaking of it here.

But the cross also means, in some places, the doctrine that Christ died for sinners upon the cross,— the atonement that He made for sinners, by His suffering for them on the cross,—the complete and perfect sacrifice for sin which He offered up, when He gave His own body to be crucified. In short, this one word, "the Cross," stands for Christ crucified, the only Saviour. This is the meaning in which Paul uses the expression, when he tells the Corinthians, " the preaching of the cross is to them that perish foolishness." (1 Cor. i. 18.) This is the meaning in which he wrote to the Galatians, " God forbid that I should glory, save in the cross." He simply meant, "I glory in nothing but Christ crucified, as the salvation of my soul." *

* "By the Cross of Christ the apostle understandeth the all-sufficient, expiatory, and satisfactory sacrifice of Christ upon the cross, with the whole work of our redemption : in the saving knowledge of, whereof he professeth he will glory and boast."—*Cudworth on Galatians.* 1613.

"Touching these words, I do not find that any expositor, either ancient or modern, Popish or Protestant, writing on this place, doth expound the cross here mentioned of the sign of the cross, but of the profession of faith in Him that was hanged on the cross."—*Mayer's Commentary.* 1631.

"This is rather to be understood of the cross which Christ suffered for us, than of that we suffer for Him."—*Leigh's Annotations.* 1650.

Reader, Jesus Christ crucified was the joy and delight, the comfort and the peace, the hope and the confidence, the foundation and the resting-place, the ark and the refuge, the food and the medicine of Paul's soul. He did not think of what he had done himself, and suffered himself. He did not meditate on his own goodness, and his own righteousness. He loved to think of what Christ had done, and Christ had suffered,—of the death of Christ, the righteousness of Christ, the atonement of Christ, the blood of Christ, the finished work of Christ. In this he did glory. This was the sun of his soul.

This is the subject he *loved to preach about.* He was a man who went to and fro on the earth, proclaiming to sinners that the Son of God had shed His own heart's blood to save their souls. He walked up and down the world, telling people that Jesus Christ had loved them, and died for their sins upon the Cross. Mark how he says to the Corinthians, "I delivered unto you first of all that which I also received, how that Christ died for our sins." (1 Cor. xv. 3.) "I determined not to know anything among you save Jesus Christ, and Him crucified." (1 Cor. ii. 2.) He, a blaspheming, persecuting Pharisee, had been washed in Christ's blood. He could not hold his peace about it. He was never weary of telling the story of the Cross.

This is the subject he *loved to dwell upon when he wrote* to believers. It is wonderful to observe how full his epistles generally are of the sufferings and death of Christ,—how they run over with "Thoughts that breathe, and words that burn," about Christ's dying love and power. His heart seems full of the subject. He enlarges on it constantly. He returns to it continually. It is the golden thread that runs through all his doctrinal teaching, and practical exhortations. He seem to think that the most advanced Christian can never hear too much about the Cross.*

This is what *he lived upon* all his life, from the time of his conversion. He tells the Galatians, "The life that I now live in the flesh I live by the faith of the Son of God, who loved me, and gave Himself for me." (Galat. ii. 20.) What made him so strong to labour? What made him so willing to work? What made him so unwearied in endeavours to save some? What made him so persevering and patient? I will tell you the secret of it all. He was always feeding by faith on Christ's body and Christ's blood. Jesus crucified was the meat and drink of his soul.

And, reader, you may rest assured that Paul was right. Depend upon it, the Cross of Christ,—the death of Christ on the cross to make atonement for sinners,—is the centre truth in the whole Bible.

---

* "Christ crucified is the sum of the Gospel, and contains all the riches of it. Paul was so much taken with Christ, that nothing sweeter than Jesus could drop from his pen and lips. It is observed that he hath the word 'Jesus' five hundred times in his Epistles."—*Charnock.* 1684.

This is the truth we begin with when we open Genesis. The seed of the woman bruising the serpent's head is nothing else but a prophecy of Christ crucified. This is the truth that shines out, though veiled, all through the law of Moses and the history of the Jews. The daily sacrifice, the passover lamb, the continual shedding of blood in the tabernacle and temple,—all these were emblems of Christ crucified. This is the truth that we see honoured in the vision of heaven before we close the book of Revelation. "In the midst of the throne and of the four beasts," we are told, "and in the midst of the elders stood a lamb as it had been slain." (Rev. v. 6.) Even in the midst of heavenly glory we get a view of Christ crucified. Take away the Cross of Christ, and the Bible is a dark book. It is like the Egyptian hieroglyphics, without the key that interprets their meaning,—curious and wonderful, but of no real use.

Reader, mark what I say. You may know a good deal about the Bible. You may know the outlines of the histories it contains, and the dates of the events described, just as a man knows the history of England. You may know the names of the men and women mentioned in it, just as a man knows Cæsar, Alexander the Great, or Napoleon. You may know the several precepts of the Bible, and admire them, just as a man admires Plato, Aristotle, or Seneca. But if you have not yet found out that Christ crucified is the foundation of the whole volume, you have read your Bible hitherto to very little profit. Your religion is a heaven without a sun, an arch without a key-stone, a compass without a needle, a clock without spring or weights, a lamp without oil. It will not comfort you. It will not deliver your soul from hell.

Reader, mark what I say again. You may know a good deal about Christ, by a kind of head knowledge. You may know who He was, and where He was born, and what He did. You may know His miracles, His sayings, His prophecies, and His ordinances. You may know how He lived, and how He suffered, and how He died. But unless you know the power of Christ's Cross by experience,— unless you know and feel within that the blood shed on that cross has washed away your own particular sins,—unless you are willing to confess that your salvation depends entirely on the work that Christ did upon the Cross,—unless this be the case, Christ will profit you nothing. The mere knowing Christ's name will never save you. You must know His Cross, and His blood, or else you will die in your sins.*

Reader, as long as you live, *beware of a religion in*

---

* "If our faith stop in Christ's life, and do not fasten upon His blood, it will not be a justifying faith. His miracles which prepared the world for His doctrines ; His holiness which fitted Himself for His sufferings, had been insufficient for us without the addition of the cross."—*Charnock.* 1684.

which there is not much of the Cross. You live in times when the warning is sadly needful. Beware, I say again, of a religion without the Cross.

There are hundreds of places of worship in this day, in which there is everything almost except the Cross. There is carved oak, and sculptured stone. There is stained glass, and brilliant painting. There are solemn services, and a constant round of ordinances. But the real Cross of Christ is not there. Jesus crucified is not proclaimed in the pulpit. The Lamb of God is not lifted up, and salvation by faith in Him is not freely proclaimed. And hence all is wrong. Reader, beware of such places of worship. They are *not apostolical.* They would not have satisfied St. Paul.*

There are thousands of religious books published in our times, in which there is everything except the Cross. They are full of directions about sacraments, and praises of the Church. They abound in exhortations about holy living, and rules for the attainment of perfection. They have plenty of fonts and crosses both inside and outside. But the real Cross of Christ is left out. The Saviour and His dying love are either not mentioned, or mentioned in an unscrip-

---

* " Paul determined to, know nothing else but Jesus Christ and Him crucified. But many manage the ministry as if they had taken up a contrary determination, even to know anything save Jesus Christ and Him crucified."—*Traill.* 1690.

tural way. And hence they are worse than useless. Reader, beware of such books. They are *not apostolical*. They would never have satisfied St. Paul.

Reader, St. Paul gloried in nothing but the Cross. Strive to be like him. Set Jesus crucified fully before the eyes of your soul. Listen not to any teaching which would interpose anything between you and Him. Do not fall into the old Galatian error. Think not that any one in this day is a better guide than the apostles. Do not be ashamed of the old paths, in which men walked who were inspired by the Holy Ghost. Let not the vague talk of men who speak great swelling words about catholicity, and the church, and the ministry, disturb your peace, and make you loose your hands from the Cross. Churches, ministers, and sacraments, are all useful in their way, but they are not Christ crucified. Do not give Christ's honour to another. "He that glorieth, let him glory in the Lord."

III. Let me show you *why all Christians ought to glory in the Cross of Christ.*

I feel that I must say something on this point, because of the ignorance that prevails about it. I suspect that many see no peculiar glory and beauty in the subject of Christ's Cross. On the contrary, they think it painful, humbling, and degrading. They do not see much profit in the story of His death and sufferings. They rather turn from it as an unpleasant thing.

Now I believe that such persons are quite wrong. I cannot hold with them. I believe it is an excellent thing for us all to be continually dwelling on the Cross of Christ. It is a good thing to be often reminded how Jesus was betrayed into the hands of wicked men.—how they condemned Him with most unjust judgment,—how they spit on Him, scourged Him, beat Him, and crowned Him with thorns,—how they led Him forth as a lamb to the slaughter, without His murmuring or resisting,—how they drove the nails through His hands and feet, and set Him up on Calvary between two thieves,—how they pierced His side with a spear, mocked Him in His sufferings, and let Him hang there naked and bleeding till He died. Of all these things, I say, it is good to be reminded. It is not for nothing that the crucifixion is described four times over in the New Testament. There are very few things that all the four writers of the Gospel describe. Generally speaking, if Matthew, Mark, and Luke tell a thing in our Lord's history, John does not tell it. But there is one thing that all the four give us most fully, and that one thing is, the story of the Cross. This is a striking fact, and not to be overlooked.

People seem to forget that all Christ's sufferings on the cross were *fore-ordained*. They did not come on

Him by chance or accident. They were all planned, counselled, and determined from all eternity. The Cross was foreseen in all the provisions of the blessed Trinity for the salvation of sinners. In the purposes of God the Cross was set up from everlasting. Not one throb of pain did Jesus feel, not one precious drop of blood did Jesus shed, which had not been appointed long ago. Infinite wisdom planned that redemption should be by the Cross. Infinite wisdom brought Jesus to the Cross in due time. He was crucified by the determinate counsel and fore-knowledge of God.

People seem to me to forget that all Christ's sufferings on the cross were *necessary to man's salvation.* He had to bear our sins, if ever they were to be borne at all. With His stripes alone could we be healed. This was the one payment of our debt that God would accept. This was the great sacrifice on which our eternal life depended. If Christ had not gone to the cross and suffered in our stead, the just for the unjust, there would not have been a spark of hope for us. There would have been a mighty gulf between ourselves and God, which no man ever could have passed.*

---

* "In Christ's humiliation stands our exaltation ; in His weakness stands our strength ; in His ignominy our glory ; in His death our life"—*Cudworth,* 1613.

"The eye of faith regards Christ sitting on the summit of the cross, as in a triumphal chariot ; the devil bound to the lowest part of the same cross, and trodden under the feet of Christ."—*Bishop Davenant on Colossians.* 1627.

People seem to me to forget that all Christ's sufferings were endured *voluntarily* and of His own free will. He was under no compulsion. Of His own choice He laid down His life. Of His own choice He went to the Cross to finish the work He came to do. He might easily have summoned legions of angels with a word, and scattered Pilate and Herod and all their armies, like chaff before the wind. But He was a willing sufferer. His heart was set on the salvation of sinners. He was resolved to open a fountain for all sin and uncleanness, by shedding His own blood.

Reader, when I think of all this, I see nothing painful or disagreeable in the subject of Christ's Cross. On the contrary, I see in it wisdom and power, peace and hope, joy and gladness, comfort and consolation. The more I keep the Cross in my mind's eye, the more fulness I seem to discern in it. The longer I dwell on the Cross in my thoughts, the more I am satisfied that there is more to be learned at the foot of the Cross than anywhere else in the world.

Would I know the length and breadth of *God the Father's love* towards a sinful world? Where shall I see it most displayed? Shall I look at His glorious sun shining down daily on the unthankful and evil? Shall I look at seed-time and harvest returning in regular yearly succession? Oh, no! I can find a stronger proof of love than anything of this sort. I look at

the Cross of Christ. I see in it not the cause of the
Father's love but the effect. There I see that God so
loved this wicked world, that He gave His only begotten Son,—gave Him to suffer and die,—that whosoever believeth in Him should not perish, but have
eternal life. I know that the Father loves us, because He did not withhold from us His Son, His only
Son. Ah, reader, I might sometimes fancy that God
the Father is too high and holy to care for such miserable, corrupt creatures as we are. But I cannot,
must not, dare not think it, when I look at the Cross
of Christ.*

Would I know how exceeding *sinful and abominable
sin is* in the sight of God? Where shall I see that
most fully brought out? Shall I turn to the history
of the flood, and read how sin drowned the world?
Shall I go to the shore of the Dead Sea, and mark
what sin brought on Sodom and Gomorrah? Shall
I turn to the wandering Jews, and observe how sin
has scattered them over the face of the earth? No!
I can find a clearer proof still. I look at the Cross
of Christ. There I see that sin is so black and dam-
nable, that nothing but the blood of God's own Son

* "The world we live in had fallen upon our heads, had it
not been upheld by the pillar of the Cross; had not Christ
stepped in and promised a satisfaction for the sin of man.
By this all things consist; not a blessing we enjoy but may
put us in mind of it; they were all forfeited by sin, but merited
by His blood. If we study it well, we shall be sensible how
God hated sin and loved a world."—*Charnock.* 1684.

can wash it away. There I see that sin has so separated me from my holy Maker, that all the angels in heaven could never have made peace between us. Nothing could reconcile us short of the death of Christ. Ah, if I listened to the wretched talk of proud men, I might sometimes fancy sin was not so very sinful. But I cannot think little of sin when I look at the Cross of Christ.*

Would I know the *fulness and completeness of the salvation* God has provided for sinners? Where shall I see it most distinctly? Shall I go to the general declarations in the Bible about God's mercy? Shall I rest in the general truth that God is a God of love? Oh, no! I will look at the Cross of Christ. I find no evidence like that. I find no balm for a sore conscience, and a troubled heart, like the sight of Jesus dying for me on the accursed tree. There I see that a full payment has been made for all my enormous debts. The curse of that law which I have broken has come down on One who there suffered in my stead. The demands of that law are all satisfied. Payment has been made for me, even to the uttermost farthing. *It will not be required twice over.* Ah, I might sometimes imagine I was too bad to be forgiven. My own heart sometimes whispers that I

* "If God hateth sin so much that He would allow neither man nor angel for the redemption thereof, but only the death of His only and well-beloved Son, who will not stand in fear thereof?"—*Church of England Homily for Good Friday.* 1560.

am too wicked to be saved. But I know in my better moments this is all my foolish unbelief. I read an answer to my doubts in the blood shed on Calvary. I feel sure that there is a way to heaven for the very vilest of men, when I look at the Cross.

Would I find strong *reasons for being a holy man?* Whither shall I turn for them? Shall I listen to the ten commandments merely? Shall I study the examples given me in the Bible of what grace can do? Shall I meditate on the rewards of heaven, and the punishments of hell? Is there no stronger motive still? Yes! I will look at the Cross of Christ. There I see the love of Christ constraining me to live not unto myself, but unto Him. There I see that I am not my own now;—I am bought with a price. I am bound by the most solemn obligations to glorify Jesus with body and spirit, which are His. There I see that Jesus gave Himself for me not only to redeem me from all iniquity, but also to purify me, and make me one of a peculiar people, zealous of good works. He bore my sins in His own body on the tree, that I being dead unto sin should live unto righteousness. Ah, reader, there is nothing so sanctifying as a clear view of the Cross of Christ. It crucifies the world unto us, and us unto the world How can we love sin when we remember that because of our sins Jesus died? Surely none ought to be so holy as the disciples of a crucified Lord.

Would I *learn how to be contented and cheerful* under all the cares and anxieties of life? What school shall I go to? How shall I attain this state of mind most easily? Shall I look at the sovereignty of God, the wisdom of God, the providence of God, the love of God? It is well to do so. But I have a better argument still. I will look at the Cross of Christ. I feel that He who spared not His only begotten Son, but delivered Him up to die for me, will surely with Him give me all things that I really need. He that endured that pain for my soul, will surely not withhold from me anything that is really good. He that has done the greater things for me, will doubtless do the lesser things also. He that gave His own blood to procure me a home in heaven, will unquestionably supply me with all that is really profitable for me during my journey through the world. Ah, reader, there is no school for learning contentment that can be compared with the foot of the Cross.

Would I gather *arguments for hoping that I shall never be cast away?* Where shall I go to find them? Shall I look at my own graces and gifts? Shall I take comfort in my own faith, and love, and penitence, and zeal, and prayer? Shall I turn to my own heart and say, "This same heart will never be false and cold"? Oh, no! God forbid! I will look at the Cross of Christ. This is my grand argument. This is my main stay. I cannot think that He who went through such sufferings to redeem my soul, will let that soul perish after all, when it has once cast itself on Him. Oh, no! what Jesus paid for, Jesus will surely keep. He paid dearly for it. He will not let it easily be lost. He died for me when I was yet a dark sinner. He will never forsake me after I have believed. Ah, reader, when Satan tempts you to doubt whether Christ's people will be kept from falling, you should tell Satan to look at the Cross."*

And now, reader, will you marvel that I said all Christians ought to glory in the Cross? Will you not rather wonder that any can hear of the Cross and remain unmoved? I declare I know no greater proof of man's depravity, than the fact that thousands of so-called Christians see nothing glorious in the Cross. Well may our hearts be called stony,— well may the eyes of our mind be called blind,—well may our whole nature be called diseased,—well may we all be called dead, when the Cross of Christ is heard of, and yet neglected. Surely we may take up the words of the prophet, and say, "Hear O heavens, and be astonished O earth; a wonderful

---

* "The believer is so freed from eternal wrath, that if Satan and conscience say, 'Thou art a sinner, and under the curse of the law,' he can say, 'It is true, I am a sinner, but I was hanged on a tree and died, and was made a curse in my Head, and Lawgiver, Christ, and His payment and suffering is my payment and suffering.'"—*Rutherford's Christ Dying.* 1647.

and a horrible thing is done,"—Christ was crucified for sinners, and yet many Christians live as if He was never crucified at all!

Reader, the Cross is *the grand peculiarity of the Christian religion*. Other religions have laws and moral precepts,—forms and ceremonies,—rewards and punishments. But other religions cannot tell us of a dying Saviour. They cannot show us the Cross. This is the crown and glory of the Gospel. This is that special comfort which belongs to it alone. Miserable indeed is that religious teaching which calls itself Christian, and yet contains nothing of the Cross. A man who teaches in this way, might as well profess to explain the solar system, and yet tell his hearers nothing about the sun.

The Cross is *the strength of a minister*. I for one would not be without it for the world. I should feel like a soldier without arms,—like an artist without his pencil,—like a pilot without his compass,—like a labourer without his tools. Let others, if they will, preach the law and morality. Let others hold forth the terrors of hell, and the joys of heaven. Let others drench their congregations with teachings about the sacraments and the Church. Give me the Cross of Christ. This is the only lever which has ever turned the world upside down hitherto, and made men forsake their sins. And if this will not, nothing will. A man may begin preaching with a

perfect knowledge of Latin, Greek, and Hebrew.
But he will do little or no good among his hearers
unless he knows something of the Cross. Never was
there a minister who did much for the conversion of
souls who did not dwell much on Christ crucified.
Luther, Rutherford, Whitefield, M'Cheyne, were all
most eminent preachers of the Cross. This is the
preaching that the Holy Ghost delights to bless. He
loves to honour those who honour the Cross.

The Cross is *the secret of all missionary success.* Nothing but this has ever moved the hearts of the
heathen. Just according as this has been lifted up
missions have prospered. This is the weapon that
has won victories over hearts of every kind, in every
quarter of the globe. Greenlanders, Africans, South-
Sea Islanders, Hindoos, Chinese, all have alike felt
its power. Just as that huge iron tube which crosses
the Menai Straits, is more affected and bent by half
an hour's sunshine than by all the dead weight that
can be placed in it, so in like manner the hearts of
savages have melted before the Cross when every
other argument seemed to move them no more than
stones. "Brethren," said a North American Indian,
after his conversion, "I have been a heathen. I
know how heathens think. Once a preacher came
and began to explain to us that there was a God;
but we told him to return to the place from whence
he came. Another preacher came and told us not to

lie, nor steal, nor drink; but we did not heed him.
At last another came into my hut one day, and said,
'I am come to you in the name of the Lord of heaven
and earth. He sends to let you know that He will
make you happy, and deliver you from misery. For
this end He became a man, gave His life a ransom,
and shed His blood for sinners.' I could not forget
his words. I told them to the other Indians, and an
awakening begun among us. I say therefore preach
the sufferings and death of Christ our Saviour, if
you wish your words to gain entrance among the
heathen." Never indeed did the devil triumph so
thoroughly as when he persuaded the Jesuit missionaries in China to keep back the story of the Cross.

The Cross is *the foundation of a Church's prosperity*.
No Church will ever be honoured in which Christ
crucified is not continually lifted up. Nothing
whatever can make up for the want of the Cross.
Without it all things may be done decently and in
order. Without it there may be splendid ceremonies, beautiful music, gorgeous churches, learned
ministers, crowded communion tables, huge collections for the poor. But without the Cross no good
will be done. Dark hearts will not be enlightened.
Proud hearts will not be humbled. Mourning hearts
will not be comforted. Fainting hearts will not be
cheered. Sermons about the catholic Church and an
apostolic ministry,—sermons about baptism and the

Lord's Supper,—sermons about unity and schism,—
sermons about fasts and communion,—sermons about
fathers and saints,—such sermons will never make
up for the absence of sermons about the Cross of
Christ. They may amuse some. They will feed
none. A gorgeous banqueting room and splendid
gold plate on the table, will never make up to a
hungry man for the want of food. Christ crucified
is God's grand ordinance for doing good to men.
Whenever a Church keeps back Christ crucified,
or puts anything whatever in that foremost place
which Christ crucified should always have, from that
moment a Church ceases to be useful. Without
Christ crucified in its pulpits, a Church is little better
than a cumberer of the ground, a dead carcase, a
well without water, a barren fig tree, a sleeping
watchman, a silent trumpet, a dumb witness, an
ambassador without terms of peace, a messenger
without tidings, a lighthouse without fire, a stum-
bling-block to weak believers, a comfort to infidels,
a hot-bed for formalism, a joy to the devil, and an
offence to God.

The Cross is *the grand centre of union* among true
Christians. Our outward differences are many, with-
out doubt. One man is an Episcopalian, another is a
Presbyterian,—one is an Independent, another a
Baptist,—one is a Calvinist, another an Armenian,—
one is a Lutheran, another a Plymouth Brother,—

one is a friend to establishments, another a friend to the voluntary system,—one is a friend to liturgies, another a friend to extempore prayer. But, after all, what shall we hear about most of these differences in heaven? Nothing most probably: nothing at all. *Does a man really and sincerely glory in the Cross of Christ?* That is the grand question. If he does, he is my brother:—we are travelling on the same road. We are journeying towards a home where Christ is all, and everything outward in religion will be forgotten. But if he does not glory in the Cross of Christ, I cannot feel comfort about him. Union on outward points only is union only for time. —Union about the Cross is union for eternity. Error on outward points is only a skin-deep disease.—Error about the Cross is disease at the heart. Union about outward points is a mere man-made union.—Union about the Cross of Christ can only be produced by the Holy Ghost.

Reader, I know not what you think of all this. I feel as if I had said nothing compared to what might be said. I feel as if the half of what I desired to tell you about the Cross were left untold. But I do hope that I have given you something to think about. I do trust that I have shown you that I have reason for the question with which I began this volume, "What do you think and feel about the Cross of Christ?" Listen to me now for a few moments,

while I say something to apply the whole subject to
your conscience.

Are you living in any kind of sin? Are you following the course of this world, and neglecting your
soul? Hear, I beseech you, what I say to you this
day: "Behold the Cross of Christ." See there how
Jesus loved you! See there what Jesus suffered to
prepare for you a way of salvation! Yes: careless
men and women, for you that blood was shed! For
you those hands and feet were pierced with nails!
For you that body hung in agony on the Cross! You
are they whom Jesus loved, and for whom He died!
Surely that love ought to melt you. Surely the
thought of the Cross should draw you to repentance.
Oh, that it might be so this very day! Oh, that
you would come at once to that Saviour who died for
you, and is willing to save. Come and cry to Him
with the prayer of faith, and I know that He will
listen. Come and lay hold upon the Cross, and I
know that He will not cast you out. Come and
believe on Him who died on the Cross, and this very
day you shall have eternal life. How will you ever
escape, if you neglect so great salvation? None surely
will be so deep in hell as those who despise the Cross!

Are you inquiring the way towards heaven? Are you
seeking salvation, but doubtful whether you shall
find it? Are you desiring to have an interest in
Christ, but doubting whether Christ will receive

you? To you also I say this day, "Behold the
Cross of Christ." Here is encouragement if you
really want it. Draw near to the Lord Jesus with
boldness, for nothing need keep you back. His arms
are open to receive you. His heart is full of love
towards you. He has made a way by which you
may approach Him with confidence. Think of the
Cross. Draw near, and fear not.

Are you an unlearned man? Are you desirous to
get to heaven, and yet perplexed and brought to
a stand-still by difficulties in the Bible which you
cannot explain? To you also I say this day, "Behold the Cross of Christ." Read there the Father's
love and the Son's compassion. Surely they are
written in great plain letters, which none can well
mistake. What though you are now perplexed by
the doctrine of election? What though at present
you cannot reconcile your own responsibility? Look,
I say, at the Cross. Does not that Cross tell you
that Jesus is a mighty, loving, ready Saviour? Does
it not make one thing plain, and that is, that if not
saved it is all your own fault? Oh, get hold of that
truth, and hold it fast!

Are you a distressed believer? Is your heart pressed
down with sickness, tried with disappointments, over-
burdened with cares? To you also I say this day,
"Behold the Cross of Christ." Think whose hand
it is that chastens you. Think whose hand is mea-

suring to you the cup of bitterness which you are now drinking. It is the hand of Him that was crucified. It is the same hand that in love to your soul was nailed to the accursed tree. Surely that thought should comfort and hearten you. Surely you should say to yourself, "A crucified Saviour will never lay upon me anything that is not for my good. There is a needs be. It must be well."

Are you a believer that longs to be more holy? Are you one that finds his heart too ready to love earthly things? To you also I say, "Behold the Cross of Christ." Look at the Cross. Think of the Cross. Meditate on the Cross, and then go and set your affections on the world if you can. I believe that holiness is nowhere learned so well as on Calvary. I believe you cannot look much at the Cross without feeling your will sanctified, and your tastes made more spiritual. As the sun gazed upon makes everything else look dark and dim, so does the Cross darken the false splendour of this world As honey tasted makes all other things seem to have no taste at all, so does the Cross, seen by faith, take all the sweetness out of the pleasures of the world. Keep on every day steadily looking at the Cross of Christ, and you will soon say of the world as the poet does, —

> Its pleasures now no longer please,
>   No more content afford ;
> Far from my heart be joys like these,
>   Now I have seen the Lord.

As by the light of opening day
The stars are all concealed,
So earthly pleasures fade away
When Jesus is revealed.

Are you a dying believer? Have you gone to that
bed from which something within tells you you will
never come down alive? Are you drawing near to
that solemn hour when your soul and body must
part for a season, and you must launch into a world
unknown? Oh, look steadily at the Cross of Christ,
and you shall be kept in peace. Fix the eyes of your
mind firmly on Jesus crucified, and He shall deliver
you from all your fears. Though you walk through
dark places, He will be with you. He will never
leave you, never forsake you. Sit under the shadow
of the Cross to the very last, and its fruit shall be
sweet to your taste. "Ah!" said a dying missionary,
"there is but one thing needful on a death-bed, and
that is to feel one's arm around the Cross."

Reader, I lay these thoughts before your mind.
What you think now about the Cross of Christ I
cannot tell; but I can wish you nothing better than
this, that you may be able to say with the apostle
Paul, before you die or meet the Lord, "God forbid
that I should glory, save in the Cross of our Lord
Jesus Christ."

I remain,

Your affectionate friend,

J. C. RYLE

"Where art Thou?"

READER,

  The question before your eyes is the first
which God asked of man after the fall. It is the
question He put to Adam in the day that he ate the
forbidden fruit, and became a sinner.

In vain did Adam and his wife hide themselves
among the trees of the garden of Eden. In vain
did they try to escape the eye of the all-seeing God.
They heard the voice of the Lord God, walking in
the cool of the day: "And the Lord God called unto
Adam, and said unto him, Where art thou?" (Gen.
iii. 9.) Think for a moment how awful those words
must have sounded! Think what the feelings of
Adam and Eve must have been!

Reader, 6,000 years have well-nigh passed away
since this question was first asked. Millions of Adam's

children have lived and died, and gone to their own place. Millions are yet upon earth, and every one of them has a soul to be lost or saved. But no question ever has been, or even can be asked more solemn than that which is before you : Where art thou? *Where art thou in the sight of God?*—Come now, and give me your attention, while I tell you a few things which may throw light upon this question.

I know not who you are,—whether you are a Churchman or a Dissenter ;—whether you are learned or unlearned ;—whether you are rich or poor ;— whether you are old or young : about all this I know nothing. But I do know that you have got an immortal soul, and I want that soul to be saved. I do know that you have got to stand before the judgment seat of God, and I want you to be prepared for it. I do know that you will be for ever in heaven or hell, and I want you to escape hell, and reach heaven. I do know that the Bible contains most solemn things about the inhabitants of the earth, and I want every man, woman, and child in the world to hear them. I believe every word in the Bible; and because I believe it, I ask every reader of this paper, " *Where art thou in the sight of God?* "

I. In the first place, there are many people about whom the Bible shows me *I ought to be exceedingly afraid.* Reader, art thou one of them ?

These are they, who, if Bible words mean anything, have not yet been converted and born again. They are not justified. They are not sanctified. They have not the Spirit. They have no faith. They have no grace. Their sins are not forgiven. Their hearts are not changed. They are not ready to die. They are not meet for heaven. They are neither godly, nor righteous, nor saints. If they are, Bible words mean nothing at all.

Some of these persons, to all appearance, think no more about their souls than the beasts that perish. There is nothing to show that they think of a life to come any more than the horse and ox, which have no understanding. Their treasure is evidently all on earth. Their good things are plainly all on this side of the grave. Their attention is swallowed up by the perishable things of time. Meat, drink, and clothing, —money, houses, and land,—business, pleasure, or politics,—marrying, reading, or company;—these are the kind of things which fill their hearts. They live as if there were no such book as the Bible. They go on as if resurrection and eternal judgment were not true, but a lie. As to grace, and conversion, and justification, and holiness,—they are things which, like Gallio, they care not for,—they are words and names they are either ignorant of, or despise. They are all going to die. They are all going to be judged. And yet they seem to be even more hardened than the devil, for they appear neither to believe nor tremble. Alas, what a state this is for an immortal soul to be in! But oh, how common!

Some of the persons I speak of have got a form of religion, but after all it is nothing but a form. They profess and call themselves Christians. They go to a place of worship on Sunday. But when you have said that you have said all. Where is the religion of the New Testament to be seen in their lives? Nowhere at all! Sin is plainly not considered their worst enemy, nor the Lord Jesus their best friend,— nor the will of God their rule of life,—nor salvation the great end of their existence. The spirit of slumber keeps possession of their hearts, and they are at ease, self-satisfied, and content. They are in a Laodicean frame of mind, and fancy they have enough religion.

God speaks to them continually; by mercies,—by afflictions,—by Sabbaths,—by sermons; but they will not hear. Jesus knocks at the door of their hearts, but they will not open. They are told of death and eternity, and remain unconcerned. They are warned against the love of the world, and plunge into it week after week without shame. They hear of Christ coming upon earth to die for sinners, and go away unmoved. There seems a place in their hearts for everything but God;—room for business, —room for pleasures,—room for trifling,—room for sin,—room for the devil,—room for the world: but, like the inn at Bethlehem, no room for Him who made them,—no admission for Jesus, the Spirit, and the Word. Alas, what a condition of things is this! But alas, how common!

Reader, I put it solemnly to your conscience, as in the sight of God, are you one of those persons whom I have just described? There are thousands of such people in our land,—thousands in Great Britain,—thousands in Ireland,—thousands in our country parishes,—thousands in our towns,—thousands among churchmen,—thousands among dissenters,—thousands among rich,—thousands among poor. Now, are you one of them? If you are, I fear for you,—I tremble for you,—I am alarmed for you,—I am exceedingly afraid.

What is it that I fear for you? I fear everything. I fear lest you should persist in rejecting Christ till you have sinned away your own soul. I fear lest you be given over to a reprobate mind, and awake no more. I fear lest you come to such deadness and hardness of heart, that nothing but the voice of the archangel and the trump of God will break your sleep. I fear lest you cling to this vain world so closely, that nothing but death will part it and you. I fear lest you should live without Christ, die without pardon, rise again without hope, receive judgment without mercy, and sink into hell without remedy.

Reader, I must warn you, though I may seem like Lot, as one that mocks. I do solemnly warn you to flee from the wrath to come. I entreat you to remember that the Bible is all true, and must be fulfilled. —that the end of your present ways is misery and sorrow,—that without holiness no man shall see the Lord,—that the wicked shall be turned into hell, and all the people that forget God,—that God shall one day take account of all your doings, and that Christless sinners like yourself can never stand in His sight, for He is holy, and a consuming fire. Oh, that you would consider these things! Where is the man that can hold his finger for a minute in the flame of a candle? Who shall dwell with everlasting burnings?

I know well the thoughts that Satan will put into your heart, as you read these words. I know well the excuses that you are going to make. You will tell me "Religion is all very well, but a man must live." I answer, "It is quite true a man must *live*, but it is no less true that he must also *die*." You may tell me, "A man who has to work for his bread, has no time for anything else: he cannot *starve*." I answer, that "I do not want any one to starve, but neither also do I want any one to burn in hell." You may tell me, "A man must mind *his business* first in this world." I answer, "Yes! and the first business a man should mind is his eternal business, —*the business of his soul*."

Reader, I beseech you, in all affection, to break off your sins,—to repent and be converted. I beseech you to change your course;—to alter your ways about religion, to turn from your present carelessness about your soul, and become a new man. I offer to you through Jesus Christ, the forgiveness of all past sins,—free and complete forgiveness,—ready, present, everlasting forgiveness. I tell you, in my Master's name, that if you will turn to the Lord Jesus Christ, this forgiveness shall at once be your own. Oh, do not refuse so gracious an invitation! Do not hear of Christ dying for you,—Christ shedding His own blood for you,—Christ stretching out His hands to you, and yet remain unmoved. Do not love this poor perishing world better than eternal life. Dare to be bold and decided. Resolve to come out from the broad way which leads to destruction. Arise and escape for your life, while it is called to-day. Repent, believe, pray, and be saved.

Reader, I fear for you in your present state. My heart's desire and prayer is that God may teach you to fear for yourself.

II. In the second place, there are many people about whom the Bible shows me *I ought to stand in doubt*. Reader, art thou one of these?

There are many whom I must call "almost Christians," for I know no other expression in the Bible, which so exactly describes their state. They have many things about them which are right, and good, and praiseworthy, in the sight of God. They are regular and moral in their lives. They are free from glaring outward sins. They keep up many decent and proper habits. They are usually diligent in their attendance on means of grace. They appear to love the preaching of the Gospel. They are not offended at the truth as it is in Jesus, however plainly it may be spoken. They have no objection to religious company, religious books, and religious talk. They agree to all you say when you speak to them about their souls. And all this is well.

But still there is no movement in the hearts of these people that even a microscope can detect. They are like those who stand still. Weeks after weeks, years after years roll over their heads, and they are just where they were. They sit under our pulpits. They approve of our sermons. And yet, like Pharaoh's lean kine, they are nothing the better, apparently, for all they receive. There is always the same regularity about them,—the same constant attendance on means of grace,—the same wishing and hoping,—the same way of talking about religion: but there is nothing more. There is no going forward in their Christianity. There is no life, and heart, and reality in it. Their souls seem to be at a dead lock. And all this is sadly wrong.

Reader, are you one of these people? There are thousands of them in this day,—thousands in our churches, and thousands in our chapels. I ask you to give an honest answer to the question.—Is this the state of your soul in the sight of God? If it is, I can only say your condition is most unsatisfactory. As the apostle said to the Galatians, so say I unto you: "I stand in doubt of you."

How can I feel otherwise about you? There are but two sides in the world,—the side of Christ and the side of the devil; and yet you make it doubtful on which side you ought to be placed. I dare not say you are altogether careless about religion, but I cannot call you decided. I shrink from numbering you among the ungodly, but I may not place you among the Lord's children. You have some light; but is it saving knowledge? You have some feeling; but is it grace? You are not profane; but are you a man of God? You may possibly be one of the Lord's people; but you dwell so near the borders, that I cannot discern to what nation you belong. You may not perhaps be spiritually dead; but like a sickly tree in winter, I hardly know whether you are alive. And thus you live on without satisfactory evidences. I cannot help doubting about you. Surely there is a cause.

I cannot read the secrets of your hearts. Perhaps there is some pet bosom sin, which you are holding

fast and will not give up. This is a disease which
checks the growth of many a professing Christian.
Perhaps you are kept back by the fear of man: you
are afraid of the blame or laughter of your fellow-
creatures. This is an iron chain that fetters many a
soul. Perhaps you are careless about private prayer
and communion with God. This is one reason why
multitudes are weak and sickly in spirit. But whatever your reason be, I warn you in all affection to
take care what you are doing. Your state is neither
satisfactory nor safe. Like the Gibeonites, you are
found in the train of Israel, but like them you have
no title to Israel's portion, Israel's consolations, and
Israel's rewards. Oh, awake to a sense of your
danger! Strive to enter in.

Reader, you must give up this halting between two
opinions, if ever you mean to enjoy good evidences of
your salvation. There must be an alteration in you.
There must be a move. There is no real standing
still in true Christianity. If God's work is not going
forward in a man's heart, the devil's is; and if a
man is always at the same point in religion, the
probability is that he has got no religion at all. It
is not enough to wear Christ's livery; we must also
fight Christ's battles. It is not enough to cease to
do evil; we must also learn to do well. It will not
suffice to do no harm; we must also labour to do
good. Oh, tremble, lest you should prove an un-

profitable receiver of God's talents,—a barren cumberer of the ground, and your end be to be burned. Remember, he that is not with Christ, is against Him.

Reader, I charge you strongly never to rest till you have found out whether you have grace in your heart or not. Wishes, and desires, and good feelings, and convictions, are all excellent things in their way, but they alone will never save you. I like to see buds and blossoms on a tree, but I like better to see ripe fruit. The way-side hearers in the parable listened, but the Word took no root in them;—they were not saved. The stony ground hearers listened with joy, but the Word had no depth in them;—they were not saved. The thorny ground hearers brought forth something like fruit, but the Word was choked by the world;—they were not saved. Do you tremble at the Word? So also did Felix, but he was not saved. Do you like to hear good sermons, and do many things which are right? So also did Herod, but he was not saved. Do you wish to die the death of the righteous? So did Balaam, but he was not saved. Have you knowledge? So had Judas Iscariot, but he was not saved. And shall you be saved as you are? I doubt it. Remember Lot's wife.

Reader, once more I call upon you to take care what you are doing. If you will not stir up yourself to go forward, how should I feel anything but doubt about your soul?

But there are others about whom I stand in doubt, who are in worse case even than the "almost Christians." These are they who once made a high profession of religion, but have now given it up. They were once reckoned to be true believers, but they have turned back again to the world and fallen away. They have gone back from the point of religion they once seemed to have reached. They walked no more in the ways they once seemed to choose. In short, they are *backsliders*.

Reader, is this the state of your soul? If it is, know for a certainty that your condition is most unsatisfactory. It matters little what your past experience was. It proves little that you were once counted among true Christians. It may have been all a mistake and a delusion. It is your present condition of soul that I look at, and as I do so, I stand in doubt.

I believe there was a time when all the saints of God who saw you rejoiced at the sight. You seemed then to love the Lord Jesus in sincerity, and to be willing to give up the broad way for ever, and forsake all for the Gospel's sake. The Word of God appeared sweet and precious to you; the voice of Christ's ministers a most pleasant sound; the assembly of the Lord's people the place you loved best; the company of true believers your chief delight. You were never missing at the weekly meetings. Your place was never empty at Church. Your Bible was never long out of your hands. There were no days in your life without prayer. Your zeal was indeed fervent. Your religious affections were truly warm. You did run well for a season. But, oh, reader, *where, where are you now?*

You have gone back to the world. You lingered; you looked back; you returned;—I fear you had left your heart behind you. You have taken up the old man's deeds once more. You have left your first love. Your goodness has proved like the morning clouds, and as the early dew it has gone away. Your serious impressions are fast dying off; they are getting weaker and fainter every day, Your convictions are fast withering up; they are changing colour like leaves in autumn,—they will soon drop off and disappear. The gray hairs, which tell of decline, are coming here and there upon you. The preaching you once hung upon, now wearies you. The books you delighted in, give pleasure no more. The progress of Christ's Gospel is no longer interesting. The company of God's children is no longer sought. *They or you must be changed.* You are becoming shy of holy people, impatient of rebuke and advice, uncertain in your tempers, careless about little sins, not afraid of mixing with the world. *Once it was not so.* You may keep up some form of religion perhaps,— but as to vital godliness you are fast cooling down.

Already you are lukewarm; by and by you will be cold; and before long you will be icy, religion-frozen, and more dead than you were before. You are grieving the Spirit, and He will soon leave you. You are tempting the devil, and he will soon come to you; your heart is ready for him: your last state will be worse than your first. Oh, reader, strengthen the things which remain, which are ready to die. How can I possibly help feeling doubt about your soul?*

But I cannot let you go without trying to do you good. I do pity you indeed, because you are so unhappy. I know it—I am sure of it—it is useless to deny it. You have been unhappy ever since you

---

* I find that many people object to the expression, "You are grieving the Spirit, and He will soon leave you." On calm reflection I am not disposed to alter it. I think it is dangerous to attempt to be more systematic than the Bible in our theology. I think there is Scriptural warrant for saying that an unconverted man who possesses great light and knowledge in the things of religion, and yet refuses to give up sin and the world, does, in a certain sense, grieve the Holy Spirit. I would refer to Isaiah lxiii. 10; Acts vii. 51; Heb. x. 29. In taking this ground, I believe I am in entire harmony with one of the most Scriptural divines that ever lived;—I mean John Bunyan. In "Pilgrim's Progress" he represents the man in the iron cage, at the Interpreter's house, saying to Christian, "I sinned against the light of the Word, and the goodness of God. I have grieved the Spirit, and He is gone. I tempted the devil, and he is come to me. I have provoked God to anger, and He has left me."

The length to which people may go in a profession of religion, and yet remain unconverted in heart, and be lost at last, is one of the most awful and soul-searching points in theology.

fell away. You are unhappy at home, and unhappy abroad, unhappy in company, and unhappy alone; unhappy when you lie down, and unhappy when you rise up. You may have got riches, honour, love, obedience, friends; but yet *the sting* remains. There is a famine of consolation about you;—there is an utter dearth of inward peace. You are sick at heart; —you are ill at ease;—you are discontented with everybody, because you are discontented with yourself. You are like a bird that has wandered from her nest,—you never feel in your right place. You have too much religion to enjoy the world, and too little religion to enjoy God. You are weary of life, and yet afraid to die. Truly the words of Solomon are made good in your case, "You are filled with your own ways."

Reader, notwithstanding all your backslidings, there is hope even for you. There is no disease of soul that the glorious Gospel cannot cure. There is a remedy even for your case,—humbling, pride-lowering, I know,—but a sure remedy; and I earnestly beseech you to take it. That remedy is the Fountain opened for all sins,—the free mercy of God in Christ Jesus. Go and wash in that Fountain without delay, and Jesus Christ shall make thee whole.

Take down your neglected Bible and see how David fell and lay in foul sin a whole year, and yet when he repented and turned to God, there was

mercy for him. Turn to the history of the apostle
Peter, and see how he denied his Master three times
with an oath, and yet when he wept and humbled
himself, there was mercy for him. Hear what comfortable words our Lord and Saviour sends you this
day: "Come unto Me all ye that labour and are
heavy laden, and I will give you rest." "Thou hast
played the harlot with many lovers, yet, return again
to Me." "Though your sins be as scarlet, they
shall be as white as snow; though they be red like
crimson, they shall be as wool." "Return, ye backsliding children, and I will heal your backslidings."
Oh, that you may take up the words of Israel this
day, and reply, "Behold I come unto Thee, for Thou
art the Lord my God." (Matt. xi. 28; Jer. iii. 1;
Isai. i. 18; Jer. iii. 22.)

Reader, I pray God these words may not be
brought before you in vain. But remember, until
you turn from your backslidings, I must stand in
doubt about your soul.

III. In the third place, there are some people
about whom the Bible tells me *I ought to feel a good
hope.* Reader, art thou one of these?

The people I speak of have found out that they
are guilty sinners, and have fled to Christ by faith
for salvation. They have found out that sin is a
miserable and unhappy thing, and they hate it, and

long to be free from its presence altogether. In themselves they see nothing but weakness and corruption, but in the Lord Jesus they see the very things their souls require;—pardon, peace, light, comfort, and strength. Christ's blood, Christ's cross, Christ's righteousness, Christ's intercession,—these are the things on which their minds love to dwell. Their affections are now set on things above. They care for nothing so much as pleasing God. While they live their chief desire is to live to the Lord. When they die, their only desire is to die in the Lord. After death, their hope is that they shall be with the Lord.

Reader, is this the state of your soul? Do you know anything of the faith and hope, and affections, and experience, which I have just described? Do you find anything in your heart which answers to the account I have just given?—If you do, I thank God for it,—I congratulate you on your condition,—I feel a good hope about your soul.

I know well that you live in a world full of trials. You are yet in the wilderness; you are not at home. I know well that pride, and unbelief, and sloth, are continually struggling for the mastery within you. You have fightings without and fears within. I doubt not your heart is so treacherous and deceitful, that you are often sick of yourself and say, "Never was heart like mine." But, notwithstanding all this, I must hope well for your soul.

I hope, because I believe that God has begun a work in you which He will never allow to be over-thrown. Who taught you to hate sin and love Christ? Who made you come out from the world and delight in God's service? These things do not come from your own heart. Nature bears no such fruit. These things are the work of God, who where He begins, always finishes; who where He gives grace, will also give glory. Surely here is ground for hope.

I hope, because I believe you have an interest in an everlasting covenant, a covenant ordered in all things and sure. The stamp of heaven is upon you. The marks of the Lord Jesus are on your soul. Father, Son, and Holy Ghost, have all engaged to complete the salvation of your soul. There is a three-fold cord around you which never yet was broken. Surely here is ground for hope.

I hope, because you have a Saviour whose blood can cleanse from all sin,—a Saviour who invites all, and casts out none that come to Him,—a Saviour who will not break the bruised reed, nor quench the smoking flax,—a Saviour who can be touched with the feeling of your infirmities, and is not ashamed to call you brethren,—a Saviour who never alters: the same yesterday, to-day, and for ever, always able to save to the uttermost, always mighty to save. Surely here is ground for hope.

I hope, because the love of Christ is a love that passeth knowledge. So free and undeserved! So costly, even unto death! So powerful and all-conquering! So unchanging and enduring! So patient and forbearing! So tender and sympathizing! Truly our sins pass knowledge, and this is the very love our souls need. Surely here is ground for hope.

I hope, because God has given to you exceeding great and precious promises,—promises of being kept unto the end,—promises of grace for every time of need, and strength according to your day,—promises that never yet were broken, all yea and amen in Christ Jesus. Surely here is ground for hope.

Oh, reader, if you are a believer, these things are a strong foundation. If God be for you, who shall be against you? There is no condemnation to them that are in Christ Jesus. Nothing shall ever separate them from the love of God which is in Christ Jesus our Lord.

Come now, and let me tell you what I want you, and every true Christian to aim at. I want you to seek *more hope*. I want you not to rest satisfied with that little mite of confidence, which forms the whole stock of many of God's children. I want you to seek the full assurance of hope,—that lively hope which makes a man never ashamed.

I speak as a fellow-traveller in the narrow way. I speak as one who desires that his own hope may grow and increase every year that he lives, and wishes the hope of all his brethren to grow too. I know and am persuaded that I write things which are for your peace. As ever you would have few days of darkness,—as ever you would feel God's face smiling on your soul,—as ever you would have joy and peace in believing,—by all your recollections of past short-comings,—by all your desires of comfort in time to come,—I charge you, I exhort you, I beseech you to seek the full assurance of hope.

Ah, reader, if you are a true believer, you know well that we need these mutual exhortations! You and I are but children in the Lord's service, at our very best. Our souls are ever ready to cleave to the dust. There is room for improvement in us every day. Listen then, while I tell you a few things which we must never forget, if we would enjoy more hope,—which we must never lose sight of, if we would keep it when we have got it.

If we want to grow in grace, and have more hope, *we must seek more knowledge of our Lord Jesus Christ.* How little do we know of Him! Our cold affections towards Him are a witness against ourselves. Our eyes can never be open to what He is and does for us, or we should love Him more. There are some Christians whose minds seem ever running on the doctrine of sanctification, to the exclusion of every-thing else. They can argue warmly about little points of practice; yet they are cold about Christ. They live by rule, they walk strictly, they do many things, they fancy in a short time they shall be very strong. But all this time they lose sight of this grand truth,—that nothing is so sanctifying as knowledge of the Lord Jesus, and communion with Him. "Abide in Me," He says Himself, "and I in you. As the branch cannot bear fruit, except it abide in the vine; no more can ye except ye abide in Me." Christ must be the spring of our holiness, as well as the rock of our faith. Christ must be all in all. I doubt not He is precious to you that believe. Precious He ought to be, because of His offices, and precious because of His work. Precious He ought to be, for what He has done already;—He has called us, quickened us, washed us, justified us. Precious He ought to be for what He is doing even now;—strengthening us, interceding for us, sympathizing with us. Precious He ought to be for what He will do yet;—He will keep us to the end, raise us, gather us at His coming, present us faultless before God's throne, give us rest with Him in His kingdom. But oh, reader, Christ ought to be far more precious to us than He ever has been yet! I take you to record, if it were the last word of my life, I believe that nothing but the knowledge of Christ will ever feed a man's spirit. All our darkness arises from not keeping close to Him. The forms of religion are valuable as helps,—and public ordinances are profitable to strengthen us;—but it must be Christ crucified for sinners,—Christ seen with the eye of faith,—Christ present in the heart,—Christ as the bread of life, and Christ as the water of life,— this must be the doctrine we must ever cling to. Nothing else will either save, satisfy, or sanctify a sinful soul. We all need more knowledge of Christ. If we would grow in grace and hope let us begin here.

If we want to grow in grace and have more hope, we must seek *more knowledge of our own hearts*. We fancy we are acquainted with them, and we are not. The half of the sin that is in them has hitherto been hidden from our eyes. We have not the slightest idea how much they might deceive us if tried, and into what depths of Satan the very best of us might fall. But we all know by bitter experience, that by trusting our hearts we have often made sad mistakes. We have sometimes committed such errors that we have lost sight of our hope, and been ready to believe we had no grace at all. Oh, if we would be happy Christians, let us cease to put confidence in our hearts. Let us learn to expect nothing from them but weakness and feebleness. Let us cease to look to frames and feelings for our comforts. Hope built on anything within us must always be wavering and unstable.

If we want to grow in grace and have more hope,

we *must seek more holiness in life and conversation*.
This is a humbling lesson to dwell upon, but one
that·cannot be dwelt upon too much. There is an
inseparable connection between a close walk with
God, and comfort in our religion. Let this never be
forgotten. Truly the vessels in the Lord's house are
many of them very dull and dingy. When I look
around I see many things missing amongst us, which
Jesus loves. I miss the *meekness* and gentleness of
our Master: many of us are harsh, rough tempered,
and censorious, and we flatter ourselves that we are
faithful. I miss real *boldness* in confessing Christ
before men: we often think much more of the time
to be silent, than the time to speak. I miss real
humility : not many of us like to take the lowest place,
and esteem every one better than ourselves, and our
own strength perfect weakness. I miss real *charity :*
few of us have that unselfish spirit, which seeketh
not its own: there are few who are not more taken
up with their own feelings and their own happiness
than that of others. I miss real *thankfulness* of spirit :
we complain, and murmur, and fret, and brood over
the things we have not, and forget the things we
have. We are seldom content; there is generally a
Mordecai at our gate. I miss decided *separation from
the world :* the line of distinction is often rubbed out.
Many of us, like the chameleon, are always taking
the colour of our company; we become so like the

ungodly, that it strains a man's eyes to see the difference. Reader, these things ought not so to be. If we want more hope, let us be zealous of good works.

If we want to grow in grace, and have a more lively hope, *we must seek more watchfulness in seasons of prosperity.* I know no time in a believer's life, when his soul is in such real danger, as it is when all things go well with him. I know no time when a believer is so likely to contract spiritual diseases, and lay the foundation of many days of darkness and doubt in his inward man. You and I like the course of our life to run smoothly,—and it is natural to flesh and blood to do so. But you and I have little idea how perilous this smooth course is to our religion. The seeds of sickness are generally sown in health. It is the holiday time when lessons are forgotten. It is the sweet things which do harm to the children, and not the bitter. It is the world's favour which injures believers far more than the world's frown. David committed no adultery while fleeing before the face of Saul:—it was when Saul was dead and he was king in his stead, and there was peace in Israel. Christian, in "Pilgrim's Progress," did not lose his evidence while he was fighting with Apollyon:—it was when he was sleeping in a pleasant arbour, and no enemy seemed near. Oh, if we would have a lively hope, let us watch in the days of prosperity, and be sober.

If we want to grow in grace, and have a more lively hope, *we must seek more faith and contentment in time of trial.* Trial often makes a righteous man speak unadvisedly with his lips, and say and do things which rise like mist between his soul and Christ. Trial is a fire which often brings much dross to the surface of a believer's heart, and makes him say, "God has forgotten me, there is no hope for my soul; I am cast out of the Lord's sight; I do well to complain." Yet trial is the hand of a Father chastening us for our profit, however slow we may be to believe it. The rod is often sent in answer to a prayer for sanctification :—it is one of God's ways of carrying on that work of sanctification which we profess to desire. Jacob, and Joseph, and Moses, and David, all found this. Blessed are they who take patiently the Lord's medicines,—who bear the cross in silence, and say, "It is well." Afflictions well borne are spiritual promotions. Patience having a perfect work in the time of affliction, will sooner or later yield a precious harvest of inward hope.

If we would grow in grace, and have a more lively hope, we must seek *more preparedness for Christ's second coming.* I know no doctrine more sanctifying and quickening than the doctrine of Christ's second advent. I know none more calculated to draw us from the world, and to make us single-eyed, whole-hearted, and joyful Christians. But alas, how few believers live like men who wait for their Master's return! Who, that narrowly observes the ways of many believers, would ever think that they loved and longed for their Lord's appearing? Is it not true that there are many hearts among God's children which are not quite ready to receive Jesus? He would find the window barred,—the door shut, —the fires almost out;—it would be a cold and comfortless reception. Oh, believing reader, it ought not so to be! We want more of a pilgrim's spirit: we ought to be ever looking for and hastening to our home. The day of the Lord's advent is the day of rest, the day of complete redemption, the day when the family of God shall at last be all gathered together. It is the day when we shall no longer walk by faith, but by sight: we shall see the land that is far off,—we shall behold the King in His beauty. Surely we ought to be saying daily, "Come Lord Jesus, let Thy kingdom come." Oh, let us set Christ's second advent continually before our eyes! Let us say to ourselves every morning, "The Lord will soon return," and it will be good for our souls.

Lastly, if we want to grow in grace and have more hope, we must seek *more diligence about means of grace.* It is vain to suppose that our hope is not dependent in any sense on the pains we take in the use of God's appointed ordinances. It is dependent, and that to a very great extent. God has wisely ordered it so that lazy Christians seldom enjoy any assurance of their own acceptance. He tells us that we must labour, and strive, and work, to make our calling and election sure. Oh, that believers would re-member this, and lay it to heart!

I suspect that many of God's people are very lazy in their manner of using means. They know little of David's spirit, when he said, "My soul longeth and fainteth for the courts of the house of my God." I doubt whether there is much private prayer before and after sermons. Yet, remember, hearing alone is not everything: when all is said in the pulpit, only half the work is done. I doubt whether the Bible is as much read as it should be. Nothing in my own short experience has surprised me so much as the contented ignorance of Scripture which prevails among believers. I doubt whether private prayer is often made a business of as it should be. We are often satisfied to get up from our knees without having really seen or heard anything of God and His Christ. And all this is wrong. It is the diligent soul that enjoys lively hope.

Reader let us lay to heart the things that I have mentioned. Let us resolve, by God's help, to set them before us continually, to pray for them, strive after them, and endeavour to attain them.

This is the way to be *useful Christians*. The world knows little of Christ, beyond what it sees of Him in

His people. Oh, what plain clearly written epistles they ought to be! A hopeful growing believer is a walking sermon. He preaches far more than a minister does, for he preaches all the week round, shaming the unconverted, sharpening the converted, showing to all what grace can do. Such an one does good indeed by his life, and after death what great broad evidences he leaves behind him! We carry him to the grave without one unpleasant doubt! Oh, the value and the power of a growing Christian! The Lord make you and me such!

This is the way to be *happy Christians*. Happiness is the gift of God, but that there is the closest connection between full following of God and full happiness, let no man for an instant doubt. A hopeful growing believer has the witness within himself. He walks in the full light of the sun, and therefore he generally feels bright and warm. He does not quench the Spirit by continual inconsistencies, and so the fire within him seldom burns low. He has great peace, because he really loves God's law, and all that see him are obliged to allow that it is a privilege—and not a bondage—to be a Christian. Oh, the comfort of a tender conscience, a godly jealousy, a close walk with God, —a heavenly frame of mind! The Lord make us all of such a spirit.

And now, dear readers of every class to whom I have spoken, I heartily pray God to bless these pages to your souls. Whether you are one of those for whom *I fear*,—whether you are one of those about whom *I doubt*,—whether you are one of those whom *I look at with hope*, my heart's desire and prayer is, that you may lay down this book a wiser and better man than when you took it up.

We live in strange times. The world seems getting old and shaking. The shadows are long drawn. The evening appears to be coming on. The night will soon be upon us, when no man can work. Oh, that every reader of these pages would turn in upon himself while it is called to-day, and consider his own ways. Oh, that each would ask himself the question, Where am I? What am I? Where am I going? What will be the end of my present course? What is the hope of my soul?

Reader, once more I ask you not to despise my question. Think of it: consider it: pray over it. Oh, that it may take firm hold of your heart, and never leave you! Oh, that it may be to your soul as life from the dead! Time is fast ebbing away. Life is a vast uncertainty. Death is drawing nearer and nearer. Judgment is sure to come. Reader, *where art thou? Where art thou in the sight of God?*

I remain, your affectionate Friend,

J. C. RYLE

Are You Regenerate?

READER,

I wish to speak to you about Regeneration,
or being born again.

The subject is a most important one at any time.
Those words of our Lord Jesus Christ to Nicodemus
are very solemn, "Except a man be born again, he
cannot see the kingdom of God." (John iii. 3.) The
world has gone through many changes since those
words were spoken. Eighteen hundred years have
passed away. Empires and kingdoms have risen
and fallen. Great men and wise men have lived,
laboured, written, and died. But there stands the
rule of the Lord Jesus unaltered and unchanged.
And there it will stand, till heaven and earth shall
pass away: "Except a man be born again, he cannot see the kingdom of God."

But the subject is one which is doubly important in the present day. Things have happened which have drawn special attention to it. Men's minds are full of it, and men's eyes are fixed on it. Regeneration is discussed in newspayers. Regeneration is talked of in private society. Regeneration is argued about in courts of law. Surely it is a time when every true Christian should examine himself upon the subject, and make sure that his views are sound. It is a time when we should not halt between two opinions. We should try to know what we hold. We should be ready to give a reason for our belief. When the truth is assailed, those who love truth should grasp it more firmly than ever. Oh, for a greater spirit of decision throughout the land! Oh, for a more hearty determination to be always on the Lord's side!

Reader, I invite you to listen to me, while I try to bring this disputed question before you. I feel deeply that I can tell you nothing new. I know I can say nothing which has not been better said by better men than myself. But every additional witness may be of use in a disputed cause. And if I can only throw a little Scripture light on the subject of Regeneration, and make it plain to plain readers of the Bible, I shall thank God, and be abundantly satisfied. What are the opinions of men to you or me? He that judgeth us is the Lord!

One point has to be ascertained, and only one.--
"What saith the Scripture of truth?"

Now I propose to attempt three things :—

I. Firstly, to explain *what Regeneration, or being born again, means.*

II. Secondly, to show *the necessity of Regeneration.*

III. Thirdly, to point out *the marks and evidences of Regeneration.*

If the Lord God shall enable me to make these three points clear to you, I believe I shall have done your soul a great service.

I. Let me then, first of all, explain *what Regeneration, or being born again, means.*

Regeneration means, that change of heart and nature which a man goes through when he becomes a true Christian.

I think there can be no question that there is an immense difference among those who profess and call themselves Christians. Beyond all dispute, there are always two classes in the outward Church,—the class of those who are Christians in name and form only, and the class of those who are Christians in deed and in truth. All were not Israel who were called Israel, and all are not Christians who are called Christians. "In the visible Church," says an article of the Church of England, "the evil be ever mingled with the good."

Some, as the Thirty-nine Articles say, are "wicked and void of a lively faith:" others, as another article says, "are made like the image of God's only-begotten Son, Jesus Christ, and walk religiously in good works." Some worship God as a mere form, and some in spirit and in truth. Some give their hearts to God, and some give them to the world. Some believe the Bible, and live as if they believed it: others do not. Some feel their sins, and mourn over them: others do not. Some love Christ, trust in Him, and serve Him: others do not. In short, as Scripture says, some walk in the narrow way, some in the broad; some are the good fish of the Gospel net, some are the bad; some are the wheat in Christ's field, some are the tares.*

I think no man with his eyes open can fail to see all this, both in the Bible, and in the world around him. Whatever he may think about the subject I am writing of, he cannot possibly deny that this difference exists.

Now what is the explanation of the difference? I answer unhesitatingly,—Regeneration, or being born again. I answer, that true Christians are what they are, because they are Regenerate; and formal Chris-

---

* "There be two manner of men. Some there be that be not justified, nor regenerated, nor yet in the state of salvation; that is to say, not God's servants. They lack the renovation or regeneration; they be not come yet to Christ."— *Bishop Latimer's Sermons.* 1552.

tians are what they are, because they are not Regenerate. The heart of the Christian in deed has
been changed. The heart of the Christian in name
only, has not been changed. The change of heart
makes the whole difference.*

This change of heart is spoken of continually in
the Bible, under various emblems and figures.

Ezekiel calls it, "a taking away the stony heart,
and giving an heart of flesh;"—"a giving a new
heart, and putting within us a new spirit." (Ezek.
xi. 19; xxxvi. 26.)

The apostle John sometimes calls it, being "born of
God,"—sometimes, being "born again,"—sometimes,
being "born of the Spirit." (John i. 13; iii. 3—6.)

The apostle Peter, in the Acts, calls it "repenting
and being converted." (Acts iii. 19.)

The Epistle to the Romans speaks of it as a "being
alive from the dead." (Rom. vi. 13.)

The second Epistle to the Corinthians calls it
"being a new creature: old things have passed away,
and all things become new." (2 Cor. v. 17.)

* The reader must not suppose there is anything new or
modern in this statement. It would be an endless work to
quote passages from standard divines of the Church of England, in which the words "regenerate" and "unregenerate"
are used to describe the difference which I have been speaking
of. The pious and godly members of the Church are called
"the regenerate,"—the worldly and ungodly are called "the
unregenerate." I think no one, well read in English divinity,
can question this for a moment.

The Epistle to the Ephesians speaks of it as a resurrection together with Christ: "You hath He quickened who were dead in trespasses and sins" (Ephes. ii. 1); as "a putting off the old man, which is corrupt,—being renewed in the spirit of our minds,—and putting on the new man, which after God is created in righteousness and true holines." (Ephes. iv. 22, 24.)

The Epistle to the Colossians calls it a "putting off the old man with his deeds, and putting on the new man, which is renewed in knowledge after the image of Him that created him." (Coloss. iii. 9, 10.)

The Epistle to Titus calls it, "the washing of Regeneration and renewing of the Holy Ghost." (Titus iii. 5.)

The first Epistle of Peter speaks of it as "a being called out of darkness into God's marvellous light." (1 Peter ii. 9.) And the second Epistle as "being made partakers of the divine nature." (2 Peter i. 4.)

The first Epistle of John calls it a "passing from death to life." (1 John iii. 14.)

All these expressions come to the same thing in the end. They are all the same truth, only viewed from different sides. And all have one and the same meaning. They describe a great radical change of heart and nature,—a thorough alteration and transformation of the whole inner man,—a participation in the resurrection life of Christ,—or, to borrow the words of the Church of England Catechism, "a death unto sin and a new birth unto righteousness." *

This change of heart in a true Christian is so complete, that no word could be chosen more fitting to express it than that word, "Regeneration," or "new birth." Doubtless it is no outward, bodily alteration, but undoubtedly it is an entire alteration of the inner man. It adds no new faculties to a man's mind, but it certainly gives an entirely new bent and bias to all his old ones. His will is so new, his tastes so new, his opinions so new, his views of sin, the world, the Bible, and Christ so new, that he is to all intents and purposes a new man. The change seems to bring a new being into existence. It may well be called being *born again*.

This change is *not always given to believers at the same time in their lives.* Some are born again when they are infants, and seem, like Jeremiah and John the Baptist, filled with the Holy Ghost, even from their mother's womb. Some few are born again in old age. The great majority of true Christians probably are born again after they grow up. A vast multitude of persons it is to be feared, go down to the grave without having been born again at all.

This change of heart *does not always begin in the*

* "All these expressions set forth the same work of grace upon the heart, though they may be understood under different notions."—*Bishop Hopkins.* 1670.

same way in those who go through it after they have
grown up. With some, like the apostle Paul, and
the jailor at Philippi, it is a sudden and violent
change, attended with much distress of mind. With
others, like Lydia of Thyatira, it is more gentle and
gradual: their winter becomes spring almost without their knowing how. With some the change is
brought about by the Spirit working through afflictions or providential visitations. With others, and
probably the greater number of true Christians, the
Word of God, preached or written, is the means of
effecting it.*

This change is *one which can only be known and
discerned by its effects*. Its beginnings are a hidden
and secret thing. We cannot see them. Our Lord
Jesus Christ tells us this most plainly: "The wind
bloweth where it listeth, and thou hearest the sound

---

* "The preaching of the Word is the great means which
God hath appointed for Regeneration: 'faith cometh by hearing, and hearing by the Word of God.' (Rom. x. 17.) When
God first created man, it is said that 'He breathed into his
nostrils the breath of life,' but when God new creates man,
He breathes into his ears. This is the Word that raiseth the
dead, calling them out of the grave: this is that Word that
opens the eyes of the blind, that turns the heart of the dis-
obedient and rebellious. And though wicked and profane men
scoff at preaching, and count all ministers' words, and God's
words too, but so much wind, yet they are such wind, believe
it, as is able to tear rocks and rend mountains; such winds,
as if ever they are saved, must shake and overturn the foundations of all their carnal confidence and presumption. Be
exhorted, therefore, more to prize and more to frequent the
preaching of the Word."—*Bishop Hopkins.* 1670.

thereof, but canst not tell whence it cometh or whither it goeth; so is every one that is born of the Spirit." (John iii. 8.) Would you know if you are Regenerate? You must try the question, by examining what you know of the effects of Regeneration. Those effects are always the same. The ways by which true Christians are led, in passing through their great change, are certainly various. But the state of heart and soul into which they are brought at last, is always the same. Ask them what they think of sin, Christ, holiness, the world, the Bible, and prayer, and you will find them all of one mind.

This change is *one which no man can give to himself, nor yet to another.* It would be as reasonable to expect the dead to raise themselves, or to require an artist to give a marble statue life. The sons of God are "born not of blood, nor of the will of the flesh, nor of the will of man, but of God." (John i. 13.) Sometimes the change is ascribed to God the Father: "The God and Father of our Lord Jesus Christ hath begotten us again unto a lively hope." (1 Peter i. 3.) Sometimes it is ascribed to God the Son: "The Son quickeneth whom He will." (John iii. 21.) "If ye know that He is righteous, ye know that every one that doeth righteousness is born of Him." (1 John ii. 29.) Sometimes it is ascribed to the Spirit,—and He, in fact, is the great agent by whom it is always effected: "That which is born of the Spirit is Spirit."

(John iii. 6.) But man has no power to work the change. It is something far, far beyond his reach. "The condition of man after the fall of Adam," says the tenth Article of the Church of England, "is such that he cannot turn and prepare himself by his own natural strength and good works, to faith and calling upon God." No minister on earth can convey grace to any one of his congregation at his discretion. He may preach as truly and faithfully as Paul or Apollos: but God must give the increase. (1 Cor. iii. 6.) He may baptize with water in the name of the Trinity: but unless the Holy Ghost accompanies and blesses the ordinance, there is no death unto sin, and no new birth unto righteousness. Jesus alone, the great Head of the Church, can baptize with the Holy Ghost. Blessed and happy are they, who have the inward baptism, as well as the outward.*

* "The Scripture carries it, that no more than a child can beget itself, or a dead man quicken himself, or a nonentity create itself; no more can any carnal man regenerate himself, or work true saving grace in his own soul."—*Bishop Hopkins.* 1670.

"There are two kinds of baptism, and both necessary: the one interior, which is the cleansing of the heart, the drawing of the Father, the operation of the Holy Ghost: and this baptism is in man when he believeth and trusteth that Christ is the only method of his salvation."—*Bishop Hooper.* 1547.

"It is on all parts gladly confessed, that there may be, in divers cases, life by virtue of inward baptism, where outward is not found."—*Richard Hooper.* 1592.

"There is a baptism of the Spirit as of water."—*Bishop Jeremy Taylor.* 1660.

Reader, I lay before you the foregoing account of Regeneration. I say it is that change of heart which is the distinguishing mark of a true Christian man, —the invariable companion of a justifying faith in Christ,—the inseparable consequence of vital union with Him,—and the root and beginning of inward sanctification. I ask you to ponder it well before you go any further. It is of the utmost importance that your views should be clear upon this point,— *what Regeneration really is*.

I know well that many will not allow that Regeneration is what I have described it to be. They will think the statement I have made, by way of definition, much too strong. Some hold that Regeneration only means admission into a state of ecclesiastical privileges,—being made a member of the Church,—but does not mean a change of heart. Some tell us that a Regenerate man has a certain power within him which enables him to repent and believe if he thinks fit, but that he still needs a further change in order to make him a true Christian. Some say there is a difference between Regeneration and being born again. Others say there is a difference between being born again and conversion.

To all this I have one simple reply,—and that is, *I can find no such Regeneration spoken of anywhere in the Bible*. A Regeneration which only means admission into a state of ecclesiastical privileges may be ancient and primitive, for anything I know. But something more than this is wanted. A few plain texts of Scripture are needed; and these texts have yet to be found.

Such a notion of Regeneration is utterly inconsistent with that which St. John gives us in his first epistle. It renders it necessary to invent the awkward theory that there are two Regenerations, and is thus eminently calculated to confuse the minds of unlearned people, and introduce false doctrine. It is a notion which seems not to answer to the solemnity with which our Lord introduces the subject to Nicodemus. When He said, "Verily, verily, except a man be born again, he cannot see the kingdom of God," did He only mean, except a man be admitted to a state of ecclesiastical privilege? Surely He meant more than this. Such a Regeneration a man might have, like Simon Magus, and yet never be saved. Such a Regeneration He might never have, like the penitent thief, and yet see the kingdom of God. Surely He must have meant a change of heart. As to the notion that there is any distinction between being Regenerate and being born again, it is one which will not bear examination. It is the general opinion of all who know Greek, that the two expressions mean one and the same thing.

To me indeed there seems to be much confusion of ideas, and indistinctness of apprehension in men's minds on this simple point, — what Regeneration really is, — and all arising from not simply adhering to the Word of God. That a man is admitted into a state of great privilege when he is made a member of a pure Church of Christ, I do not for an instant deny. That he is in a far better and more advantageous position for his soul, than if he did not belong to the Church, I make no question. That a wide door is set open before his soul, which is not set before the poor heathen, I can most clearly see. *But I do not see that the Bible ever calls this Regeneration.* And I cannot find a single text in Scripture which warrants the assumption that it is so. It is very important in theology to distinguish things that differ. Church privileges are one thing. Regeneration is another. I, for one, dare not confound them.*

I am quite aware that great and good men have clung to that low view of Regeneration, to which I have adverted. † But when a doctrine of the everlasting Gospel is at stake, I can call no man master.

---

* "The mixture of those things by speech, which by nature are divided, is the mother of all error."—*Hooker.* 1595.

† For instance, Bishop Davenant and Bishop Hopkins frequently speak of "a sacramental Regeneration," when they are handling the subject of baptism, as a thing entirely distinct from spiritual Regeneration. The general tenor of their writings is to speak of the godly as the regenerate, and the ungodly as the unregenerate. But with every feeling of respect for two such good men, the question yet remains,—What Scripture warrant have we for saying there are two Regenerations? I answer unhesitatingly,—We have none at all.

The words of the old philosopher are never to be forgotten: "I love Plato, I love Socrates, but I love truth better than either." I say unhesitatingly, that those who hold the view that there are two Regenerations, can bring forward no plain text in proof of it. I firmly believe that no plain reader of the Bible only, would ever find this view there for himself; and that goes very far to make me suspect it is an idea of man's invention. The only Regeneration that I can see in Scripture is, not a change of *state*, but a change of *heart*. That is the view, I once more assert, which the Church Catechism takes when it speaks of the "death unto sin, and new birth unto righteousness," and on that view I take my stand.

Reader, the doctrine before you is one of vital importance. This is no matter of names, and words, and forms, about which I am writing, and you are reading. It is a thing that you and I must feel and know by experience, each for himself, if we are to be saved. Try, I beseech you, to become acquainted with it. Let not the din and smoke of controversy draw off your attention from your own heart. Is that heart changed? Alas, it is poor work to wrangle, and argue, and dispute about Regeneration, if after all we know nothing about it within.

Reader, Regeneration, or new birth, is the distinguishing mark of every true Christian. Now just consider what I say. *Are you Regenerate, or are you not?*

II. Let me show you, in the second place, *the necessity there is for our being Regenerated, or born again.*

That there is such a necessity is most plain from our Lord Jesus Christ's words in the third chapter of St. John's Gospel. Nothing can be more clear and positive than His language to Nicodemus: "Except a man be born again, he cannot see the kingdom of God." "Marvel not that I said unto thee, Ye must be born again." (John iii. 7.)

The reason of this necessity is the exceeding sinfulness and corruption of our natural hearts. The words of St. Paul to the Corinthians are literally accurate: "The natural man receiveth not the things of the Spirit of God, for they are foolishness unto him." (1 Cor. ii. 14.) Just as rivers flow downward, and sparks fly upward, and stones fall to the ground, so does a man's heart naturally incline to what is evil. We love our soul's enemies,—we dislike our soul's friends. We call good evil, and we call evil good. We take pleasure in ungodliness, we take no pleasure in Christ. We not only commit sin, but we also love sin. We not only need to be cleansed from the guilt of sin, but we also need to be delivered from its power. The natural tone, bias, and current, of our minds, must be completely altered. The image of God, which sin has blotted out, must be restored. The disorder and confusion which reigns within us must be put down. The first things must no longer be last, and the last first. The Spirit must let in the light on our hearts, put everything in its right place, and create all things new.

It ought always to be remembered that there are two distinct things which the Lord Jesus Christ does for every sinner whom He undertakes to save. He washes him from his sins in His own blood, and gives him a free pardon:—*this is his justification.* He puts the Holy Spirit into his heart, and makes him an entire new man:—*this is his Regeneration.*

The two things are *both absolutely necessary to salvation.* The change of heart is as necessary as the pardon; and the pardon is as necessary as the change. Without the pardon we have no right or title to heaven. Without the change we should not be meet and ready to enjoy heaven, even if we got there.

The two things are *never separate.* They are never found apart. Every justified man is also a Regenerate man, and every Regenerate man is also a justified man. When the Lord Jesus Christ gives a man remission of sins, He also gives him repentance. When He grants peace with God, He also grants power to become a son of God. There are two great standing maxims of the glorious Gospel, which ought never to be forgotten. One is, "He that believeth not shall be damned." (Mark xvi. 16.) The other is, "If any man have not the Spirit of Christ, he is none of His." (Rom. viii. 9.)

Reader, the man who denies the universal necessity of Regeneration, can know very little of the heart's corruption. He is blind indeed who fancies that pardon is all we want in order to get to heaven, and does not see that pardon without a change of heart would be a useless gift. Blessed be God that both are freely offered to us in Christ's Gospel, and that Jesus is able and willing to give the one as well as the other.

Surely you must be aware that the vast majority of people in the world *see nothing, feel nothing, and know nothing in religion as they ought.* How and why is this, is not the present question. I only put it to your conscience,—is it not the fact?

Tell them of the sinfulness of many things which they are doing continually;—and what is generally the reply? "They see no harm."

Tell them of the awful peril in which their souls are,—of the shortness of time,—the nearness of eternity,—the uncertainty of life,—the reality of judgment. "They feel no danger."

Tell them of their need of a Saviour,—mighty, loving, and divine, and of the impossibility of being saved from hell, except by faith in Him. It all falls flat and dead on their ears. "They see no such great barrier between themselves and heaven."

Tell them of holiness, and the high standard of living which the Bible requires. They cannot comprehend the need of such strictness. "They see no use in being so very good."

There are thousands and tens of thousands of such people on every side of us. They will hear these things all their lives. They will even attend the ministry of the most striking preachers, and listen to the most powerful appeals to their consciences. And yet, when you come to visit them on their death-beds, they are like men and women who never heard these things at all. They know nothing of the leading doctrines of the Gospel by experience. They can render no reason whatever of their own hope.

And why and wherefore is all this? What is the explanation —what is the cause of such a state of things? It all comes from this,—that man naturally has no sense of spiritual things. In vain the sun of righteousness shines before him:—the eyes of his soul are blind, and cannot see. In vain the music of Christ's invitations sounds around him :—the ears of his soul are deaf and cannot hear it. In vain the wrath of God against sin is set forth:—the perceptions of his soul are stopped up.—like the sleeping traveller, he does not perceive the coming storm. In vain the bread and water of life are offered to him : —his soul is neither hungry for the one, nor thirsty for the other. In vain he is advised to flee to the Great Physician:—his soul is unconscious of its disease:—why should he go? In vain you put a price

into his hand to buy wisdom:—the mind of his soul
wanders; he is like the lunatic who calls straws a
crown, and dust diamonds,—he says, "I am rich,
and increased with goods, and have need of nothing."
Ah, reader, there is nothing so sad as the utter corruption of our nature! There is nothing so painful
as the anatomy of a dead soul.

Now what does such a man need? He needs to be
born again, and made a new creature. He needs a
complete putting off the old man, and a complete
putting on the new. We do not live our natural life
till we are born into the world, and we do not live
our spiritual life till we are born of the Spirit.

But, reader, you must furthermore be aware that
the vast majority of people *are utterly unfit to enjoy
heaven in their present state.* I lay it before you as a
great fact. Is it not so?

Look at the masses of men and women gathered
together in our cities and towns, and observe them
well. They are all dying creatures,—all immortal
beings,—all going to the judgment seat of Christ,—
all certain to live for ever in heaven or in hell. But
where is the slightest evidence that most of them are
in the least degree meet and ready for heaven?

Look at the greater part of those who are called
Christians, in every part throughout the land. Take
any parish you please in town or country. Take
that which you know best. What are the tastes and

pleasures of the majority of people who live there?
What do they like best, when they have a choice?
What do they enjoy most, when they can have their
own way? Observe the manner in which they spend
their Sundays. Mark how little delight they seem
to feel in the Bible and prayer. Take notice of the
low and earthly notions of pleasure and happiness,
which everywhere prevail, among young and old,
among rich and poor. Mark well these things,
and then think quietly over this question: "What
would these people do in heaven?"

You and I, it may be said, know little about
heaven. Our notions of heaven may be very dim
and indistinct. But at all events, I suppose we are
agreed in thinking that heaven is a very holy place,
—that God is there,—and Christ is there,—and saints
and angels are there,—that sin is not there in any
shape,—and that nothing is said, thought, or done,
which God does not like. Only let this be granted,
and then I think there can be no doubt the great
majority of people around us are as little fit for
heaven as a bird for swimming beneath the sea, or a
fish for living upon dry land.*

* "Tell me, thou that in holy duties, grudgest at every
word that is spoken; that thinkest every summons to the
public worship as unpleasant as the sound of thy passing bell;
that sayest, 'When will the Sabbath be gone, and the ordinances be over?' What wilt thou do in heaven? What shall
such an unholy heart do there, where a Sabbath shall be as
long as eternity itself; where there shall be nothing but holy

And what is it they need in order to make them fit to enjoy heaven? They need to be Regenerated or born again. It is not a little changing and outward amendment they require. It is not merely the putting a restraint on raging passions, and the quieting of unruly affections. All this is not enough. Old age, —the want of opportunity for indulgence,—the fear of man, may produce all this. The tiger is still a tiger, even when he is chained; and the serpent is still a serpent, even when he lies motionless and coiled up. The alteration needed is far greater and deeper. They must every one have a new nature put within them. They must every one be made new creatures. The fountain-head must be purified. The root must be set right. Each one wants a new heart and a new will. The change required is not that of the snake, when he casts his skin and yet remains a reptile still. It is the change of the caterpillar, when he dies and his crawling life ceases, but from his body rises the butterfly,—a new animal, with a new nature.

All this, and nothing less, is required. Well says

duties; and where there shall not be a spare minute, so much as for a vain thought, or an idle word? What wilt thou do in heaven, where, whatsoever thou shalt hear, see, or converse with, all is holy? And by how much more perfect the holiness of heaven is than that of the saints on earth, by so much the more irksome and intolerable would it be to wicked men, —for if they cannot endure the weak light of a star, how will they be able to endure the dazzling light of the sun itself?"— *Bishop Hopkins.*

the Homily of "Good Works:" "They be as much dead to God that lack faith, as those are to the world that lack souls."

The plain truth is, the vast proportion of professing Christians in the world have nothing whatever of Christianity, except the name. The reality of Christianity, the graces, the experience, the faith, the hopes, the life, the conflict, the tastes, the hungering and thirsting after righteousness,—all these are things of which they know nothing at all. They need to be converted as truly as any among the Gentiles to whom Paul preached, and to be turned from idols, and renewed in the spirit of their minds, as really, if not as literally. And one main part of the message which should be continually delivered to the greater portion of every congregation on earth, is this : "Ye must be born again." I write this down deliberately. I know it will sound dreadful and uncharitable in many ears. But I ask any one to take the New Testament in his hand and see what it says is Christianity, and compare that with the ways of professing Christians, and then deny the truth of what I have written, if he can.

And now let every one who reads these pages remember this grand principle of Scriptural religion : "No salvation without Regeneration,—no spiritual life without a new birth,—no heaven without a new heart."

Think not for a moment that the subject of this tract is a mere matter of controversy,—an empty question for learned men to argue about, but not one that concerns you. Away with such an idea for ever! It concerns you deeply. It touches your own eternal interests. It is a thing that you must know for yourself, feel for yourself, and experience for yourself, if you would ever be saved. No soul of man, woman, or child, will ever enter heaven without having been born again.*

And think not for one moment that this Regeneration is a change which people may go through after they are dead, though they never went through it while they were alive. Away with such a notion for ever! Now or never is the only time to be saved. Now, in this world of toil and labour,—of money-getting and business,—now you must be prepared for heaven, if you are ever to be prepared at all. Now is the only time to be justified, now the only time to be sanctified, and now the only time to be born again. So sure as the Bible is true, the man

---

* "Make sure to yourselves this great change. It is no notion that I have now preached unto you. Your natures and your lives must be changed, or, believe it, you will be found at the last day under the wrath of God. For God will not change or alter the Word that is gone out of His mouth. He hath said it,—Christ, who is the truth and Word of God, hath pronounced it,—that without the new birth, or Regeneration, no man shall inherit the kingdom of God."—*Bishop Hopkins.* 1670.

who dies without these three things, will only rise
again at the last day to be lost for ever.

You may be saved, and reach heaven without
many things which men reckon of great importance,
—without riches, without learning, without books,
without worldly comforts, without health, without
house, without land, without friends;—but *without
Regeneration you will never be saved at all.* Without
your natural birth you would never have lived, and
moved, and read this book on earth; without a new
birth you will never live and move in heaven. I
bless God that the saints in glory will be a multitude
that no man can number. I comfort myself with the
thought that, after all, there will be "much people"
in heaven. But this I know and am persuaded of
from God's Word, that of all who reach heaven, there
will not be one single individual who has not been
born again.*

"Are you born again?" I say to every one whose
eye is upon this page. Once more I repeat what I
have already said, "No salvation without a new birth."

---

* "Regeneration, or the new birth, is of absolute necessity
unto eternal life. There is no other change simply necessary,
but only this. If thou art poor, thou mayst so continue, and
yet be saved. If thou art despised, thou mayest so continue,
and yet be saved. If thou art unlearned, thou mayest so
continue, and yet be saved. Only one change is necessary.
If thou art wicked and ungodly and continuest so, Christ, who
hath the keys of heaven, who shutteth and no man openeth,
hath Himself doomed thee, that thou shalt in no wise enter
into the kingdom of God."—*Bishop Hopkins.* 1670.

III. Let me, in the third place, point out *the marks of being Regenerate, or born again.*

It is a most important thing to have clear and distinct views on this part of the subject we are considering. You have seen what Regeneration is, and why it is necessary to salvation. The next step is to find out the signs and evidences by which a man may know whether he is born again or not,—whether his heart has been changed by the Holy Spirit, or whether his change is yet to come.

Now these signs and evidences are laid down plainly for us in Scripture. God has not left us in ignorance on this point. He foresaw how some would torture themselves with doubts and questionings, and would never believe it was well with their souls. He foresaw how others would take it for granted they were Regenerate who had no right to do so at all. He has therefore mercifully provided us with a test and guage of our spiritual condition, in the First Epistle general of St. John. There He has written for our learning, what the Regenerate man is, and what the Regenerate man does,—his ways, his habits, his manner of life, his faith, his experience. Every one who wishes to possess the key to a right understanding of this subject, should thoroughly study this First Epistle of St. John.

Reader, I invite your particular attention to these marks and evidences of Regeneration, while I try to set them before you in order. Forget everything else in this volume, if you will, but do not forget this part of it. I might easily mention other evidences besides those I am about to mention. But I will not do so. I would rather confine myself to the First Epistle of St. John, because of the peculiar explicitness of its statements about the man that is born of God. He that hath an ear let him hear what the beloved Apostle says about the marks of Regeneration.

1. First of all, St. John says, "Whosoever is born of God doth not commit sin;" and again, "Whosoever is born of God sinneth not." (1 John iii. 9; v. 18.)

A Regenerate man *does not commit sin as a habit.* He no longer sins with his heart and will, and whole inclination, as an unregenerate man does. There was probably a time when he did not think whether his actions were sinful or not, and never felt grieved after doing evil. There was no quarrel between him and sin: they were friends. Now he hates sin, flees from it, fights against it, counts it his greatest plague, groans under the burden of its presence, mourns when he falls under its influence, and longs to be delivered from it altogether. In one word, sin no longer pleases him, nor is even a matter of indifference: it has become the abominable thing which he hates. He cannot prevent it dwelling within him. "If he said he had no sin, there would be no truth in him" (1 John i. 8); but he can say that he cordially abhors it, and the great desire of his soul is not to commit sin at all. He cannot prevent bad thoughts arising within him, and shortcomings, omissions, and defects appearing, both in his words and actions. He knows, as St. James says, that "In many things we offend all." (James iii. 2.) But he can say truly, and as in the sight of God, that these things are a daily grief and sorrow to him, and that his whole nature does not consent unto them, as that of the unregenerate man does.

Reader, I place this mark before you. What would the Apostle say about you? Are you born of God?*

2. Secondly,—St. John says, "Whosoever believeth that Jesus is the Christ is born of God." (1 John v. 1.)

A Regenerate man believes that Jesus Christ is the only Saviour by whom his soul can be pardoned and redeemed; that He is the divine person appointed and anointed by God the Father for this very pur-

---

* "The interpretation of this place that I judge to be the most natural and unforced, is this: 'He that is born of God doth not commit sin;' that is, he doth not sin in that malignant manner in which the children of the devil do: he doth not make a trade of sin, nor live in the constant and allowed practice of it. There is a great difference betwixt regenerate and unregenerate persons in the very sins that they commit. All indeed sin; but a child of God cannot sin,—that is, though he doth sin, yet he cannot sin after such a manner as wicked and unregenerate men do."—*Bishop Hopkins.* 1670.

pose, and that beside Him there is no Saviour at all. In himself he sees nothing but unworthiness, but in Christ he sees ground for the fullest confidence, and trusting in Him, he believes that his sins are all forgiven and his iniquities all put away. He believes that for the sake of Christ's finished work and death upon the cross, he is reckoned righteous in God's sight, and may look forward to death and judgment without alarm. He may have his doubts and fears. He may sometimes tell you he feels as if he had no faith at all. But ask him whether he is willing to trust in anything instead of Christ, and see what he will say. Ask him whether he will rest his hopes of eternal life on his own goodness, his own amendments, his prayers, his minister, his doings in Church and out of Church, either in whole or in part, and see what he will reply. Ask him whether he will give up Christ, and place his confidence in any other way of salvation. Depend upon it he would say, that though he does feel weak and bad, he would not give up Christ for all the world. Depend upon it he would say he found a preciousness in Christ, a suitableness to his own soul in Christ, that he found no where else, and that he must cling to Him.

Reader, I place this mark also before you. What would the Apostle say about you? Are you born of God?

3. Thirdly,—St. John says, "Every one that doeth righteousness is born of Him." (1 John ii. 29.)

The Regenerate man is a *holy man*. He endeavours to live according to God's will, to do the things that please God, to avoid the things that God hates. His aim and desire is to love God with heart and soul, and mind and strength, and to love his neighbour as himself. His wish is to be continually looking to Christ as his example as well as his Saviour, and to show himself Christ's friend by doing whatsoever Christ commands. No doubt he is not perfect. None will tell you that sooner than himself. He groans under the burden of indwelling corruption cleaving to him. He finds an evil principle within him constantly warring against grace, and trying to draw him away from God. But he does not consent to it, though he cannot prevent its presence. In spite of all short-comings, the average bent and bias of his ways is holy,—his doings holy,—his tastes holy,—and his habits holy. In spite of all his swerving and turning aside, like a ship beating up against a contrary wind, the general course of his life is in one direction.—toward God and for God. And though he may sometimes feel so low that he questions whether he is a Christian at all, in his calmer moments he will generally be able to say, with old John Newton, "I am not what I ought to be, I am not what I want to be, I am not what I hope to be in another world, but still I am not what I once used to be, and by the grace of God I am what I am." *

Reader, I place this mark also before you. What would the Apostle say about you? Are you born of God?

4. Fourthly.—St. John says, " We know that we have passed from death unto life, because we love the brethren." (1 John iii. 14.)

A Regenerate man *has a special love for all true disciples of Christ*. Like his Father in heaven, he loves all men with a great general love, but he has a special love for them who are of one mind with himself. Like his Lord and Saviour, he loves the worst of sinners, and could weep over them; but he has a peculiar love for those who are believers. He is never so much at home as when he is in their company. He is never so happy as when he is among the saints and the excellent of the earth. Others may value learning, or cleverness, or agreeableness, or riches, or rank, in the society they choose. The Regenerate man values grace. Those who have most grace, and are most like Christ, are those he loves most. He feels that they are members of the same

---

* "Let none conclude that they have no grace, because they have many imperfections in their obedience. Thy grace may be very weak and imperfect, and yet thou mayest be truly born again to God, and be a genuine son and heir of heaven."—*Bishop Hopkins.* 1670.

family with himself, his brethren, his sisters, children of the same Father. He feels that they are fellow-soldiers fighting under the same captain, warring against the same enemy. He feels that they are his fellow-travellers, journeying along the same road, tried by the same difficulties, and soon about to rest with him in the same eternal home. He understands them, and they understand him. There is a kind of spiritual freemasonry between them. He and they may be very different in many ways,—in rank, in station, in wealth. What matter? They are Jesus Christ's people. They are his Father's sons and daughters. Then he cannot help loving them?

Reader, I place this mark also before you. What would the Apostle say about you? Are you born of God?

5. Fifthly.—St. John says, "Whatsoever is born of God overcometh the world." (1 John v. 4.)

A Regenerate man *does not make the world's opinion his rule of right and wrong.* He does not mind going against the stream of the world's ways, notions, and customs. "What will men say?" is no longer a turning point with him. He overcomes the love of the world. He finds no pleasure in things which most around him call happiness. He cannot enjoy their enjoyments: they weary him; they appear to him vain, unprofitable, and unworthy of an immortal being. He overcomes the fear of the world. He is content to do many things which all around him think unnecessary, to say the least. They blame him:—it does not move him. They ridicule him:— he does not give way. He loves the praise of God more than the praise of man. He fears offending Him more than giving offence to man. He has counted the cost. He has taken his stand. It is a small thing with him now whether he is blamed or praised. His eye is upon Him that is invisible. Him he is resolved to follow whithersoever he goeth. It may be necessary in this following to come out from the world and be separate. The Regenerate man will not shrink from doing so. Tell him that he is unlike other people, that his views are not the views of society generally, and that he is making himself singular and peculiar:—you will not shake him. He is no longer the servant of fashion and custom. To please the world is quite a secondary consideration with him. His first aim is to please God.

Reader, I place this mark also before you. What would the Apostle say about you? Are you born of God?

6. Sixthly.—St. John says, "He that is begotten of God keepeth himself." (1 John v. 18.)

A Regenerate man is *very careful of his own soul.* He endeavours not only to keep clear of sin, but also to keep clear of everything which may lead to it.

He is careful about the company he keeps. He feels that evil communications corrupt the heart, and that evil is far more catching than good, just as disease is more infectious than health. He is careful about the employment of his time;—his chief desire about it is to spend it profitably. He is careful about the books he reads;—he fears getting his mind poisoned by mischievous writings. He is careful about the friendships he forms:—it is not enough for him that people are kind, and amiable, and good-natured: all this is very well; but will they do good to his soul? He is careful over his own daily habits and behaviour;—he tries to recollect that his own heart is deceitful, and that the world is full of wickedness, that the devil is always labouring to do him harm, and therefore he would fain be always on his guard. He desires to live like a soldier in an enemy's country, to wear his armour continually, and to be prepared for temptation. He finds by experience that his soul is ever among enemies, and he studies to be a watchful, humble, prayerful man.

Reader, I place this mark also before you. What would the Apostle say of you? Are you born of God?

Such are the six great marks of Regeneration, which God has given for our learning. Let every one who has gone so far with me, read them over with attention, and lay them to heart. I believe they were written with the view to settle the great question of the present day, and intended to prevent disputes. Once more then, I ask the reader to mark and consider them.

I know there is a vast difference in the depth and distinctness of these marks among those who are Regenerate. In some people they are faint, dim, feeble, and hardly to be discerned. You almost need a microscope to make them out. In others they are bold, sharp, clear, plain, and unmistakeable, so that he who runs may read them. Some of these marks are more visible in some people, and others are more visible in others. It seldom happens that all are equally manifest in one and the same soul. All this I am quite ready to allow.

But still, after every allowance, here we find boldly painted the six marks of being born of God. Here are certain positive things laid down by St. John, as parts of the Regenerate man's character, as plainly and distinctly as the features of a man's face. Here is an inspired Apostle writing one of the last general Epistles to the Church of Christ, telling us that a man born of God does not commit sin,—believes that Jesus is the Christ,—doeth righteousness,—loves the brethren,—overcomes the world, and keepeth himself. And more than once in the very same Epistle when these marks are mentioned, the Apostle tells us that he who has not this or that mark, is "not of God." I ask the reader to observe all this.

Now what shall we say to these things? What they can say who hold that Regeneration is only an admission to outward Church privileges, I am sure I do not know. For myself I say boldly, I can only come to one conclusion. That conclusion is, that those persons only are regenerate who have these six marks about them, and that all men and women who have not these marks, are not regenerate, are not born again. And I firmly believe that this is the conclusion to which the Apostle wished us to come.

Reader, *have you these marks?* I know not what your opinions may be on this much-disputed subject of Regeneration. I know not on which side you may rank yourself. But once for all I warn you, if you find nothing in yourself answering to the marks I have been speaking of, you have reason indeed to be afraid. Without these marks it is vain to fancy you are Scripturally regenerate. The witness of the Apostle John is clear and express, that you are not. There must be a certain family likeness between God and His children. Without it you are none of His. There must be some visible evidence of the Spirit being within you, as plain as the stamp upon gold and silver, however small. Without this evidence you are only boasting of a false gift. Show me thy faith without thy works, said the Apostle James, when he wrote against those who are content with a dead faith. Show me thy Regeneration without its fruits, is an argument that ought to be pressed home on many a conscience in the present day.

Reader, *if you have not these marks*, awake to a sense of your danger. Arise from your sleep of indifference and unconcern. Know the immense peril of hell and eternal misery in which you stand. Begin to use diligently every means by which God is ordinarily pleased to give grace to men's hearts, when they have not received it in their youth. Be diligent in hearing the Gospel preached. Be diligent in reading the Bible. Be diligent, above all, in prayer to the Lord Jesus Christ for the gift of the Holy Spirit.

If you take this course, I have every hope for you. None ever sought the Lord Jesus Christ in simplicity and sincerity, and sought in vain.

If, on the contrary, you refuse to take this course, and will continue as you are, I have little hope for you, and many fears. If the Bible be true, you are not yet born again. You will not use the most likely means to obtain this mighty blessing. What can I say but this, "the Lord have mercy upon your soul!"

Reader, *if you have these marks* I have been speaking of, be advised, and strive every year to make them more clear and plain. Let your repentance be a growing habit,—your faith an increasing faith,—your holiness a progressive holiness,—your victory over the world a more decided victory,—your love to the brethren a more hearty love,—your watchfulness over yourself a more jealous watchfulness. Take this advice, and you will never repent it. This is the way to be useful and happy in your religion. This is the way to put to silence the opposition of the enemies of truth. Let others, if they will, have Regeneration on their tongues, and nowhere else. Let it be your care to have it shining forth in your life, and to feel it in your heart.

Reader, I commend what I have been saying to your serious consideration. I believe that I have told you nothing but what is God's truth. You live in a day of gross darkness on the subject of Regeneration. Thousands are darkening God's counsel by confounding baptism and Regeneration. Beware of this. Keep the two subjects separate in your mind. Get clear views about Regeneration first of all, and then you are not likely to fall into mistakes about baptism. And when you have got clear views hold them fast, and never let them go.

∗ The reader who wishes to ascertain the true view of the Church of England on the doctrine of Regeneration, is referred to the Author's larger Work on the subject, where he will find the point fully discussed, and the objections commonly raised against the statements of the preceding pages fully considered.

Do You Pray?

"*Men ought always to pray.*"—(LUKE xviii. 1.)
"*I will that men pray everywhere.*"—(1 TIM. ii. 8.)

I OFFER you a question which deserves serious consideration. It heads the page before your eyes. It is contained in three little words,—Do you pray?

The question is one that none but you can answer. Whether you attend public worship or not, your minister knows. Whether you have family prayers in your house or not, your relations know. But whether you pray in private or not, is a matter between yourself and God.

Reader, I beseech you in all affection to attend to the subject I bring before you. Do not say that my question is too close. If your heart is right in the sight of God, there is nothing in it to make you afraid. Do not turn off my question by replying that you "say your prayers." It is one thing to say your prayers, and another to pray. Do not tell me that my question is unnecessary. Listen to me for a few minutes, and I will show you good reasons for asking it.

I. *I ask whether you pray, because prayer is absolutely needful to a man's salvation.*

I say absolutely needful, and I say so advisedly. I am not speaking now of infants and idiots. I am not settling the state of the heathen. I know that where little is given, there little will be required. I speak especially of those who call themselves Christians in a land like our own. And of such I say no man or woman can expect to be saved who does not pray.

I hold salvation by grace as strongly as any one. I would gladly offer a free and full pardon to the greatest sinner that ever lived. I would not hesitate to stand by his dying bed, and say, "Believe on the Lord Jesus Christ even now, and you shall be saved." But that a man can have salvation without *asking* for it, I cannot see in the Bible. That a man will receive pardon of his sins who will not so much as lift up his heart inwardly, and say, "Lord Jesus, give it to me," this I cannot find. I can find that nobody will be saved by his prayers, but I cannot find that without prayer anybody will be saved.

It is not absolutely needful to salvation that a man should *read* the Bible. A man may have no learning, or be blind, and yet have Christ in his heart. It is not absolutely needful that a man should *hear* the public preaching of the Gospel. He may live where the Gospel is not preached, or he may be bedridden, or deaf. But the same thing cannot be said about prayer. It is absolutely needful to salvation that a man should *pray*.

There is no royal road, either to health or learning. Princes and kings,—poor men and peasants, all alike must attend to the wants of their own bodies and their own minds. No man can eat, drink, or sleep, by proxy. No man can get the alphabet learned for him by another. All these are things which everybody must do for himself, or they will not be done at all.

Just as it is with the mind and body, so it is with the soul. There are certain things absolutely needful to the soul's health and well being. Each must attend to these things for himself. Each must repent for himself. Each must apply to Christ for himself. And for himself each must speak to God and pray. You must do it for yourself, for by no body else can it be done.

How can you expect to be saved by an "unknown"

God? And how can you know God without prayer? You know nothing of men and women in this world, unless you speak with them. You cannot know God in Christ, unless you speak to Him in prayer. If you wish to be with Him in heaven, you must be one of His friends on earth. If you wish to be one of His friends on earth, *you must pray*.

Reader, there will be many at Christ's right hand in the last day. The saints, gathered from North and South, and East and West, will be a multitude that no man can number. The song of victory that will burst from their mouths, when their redemption is at length complete, will be a glorious song indeed. It will be far above the noise of many waters, and of mighty thunders. But there will be no discord in that song. They that sing will sing with one heart, as well as one voice. Their experience will be one and the same. All will have believed. All will have been washed in the blood of Christ. All will have been born again. All will have prayed. Yes: we must pray on earth, or we shall never praise in heaven. We must go through the school of prayer, or we shall never be fit for the holiday of praise.

Reader, to be prayerless is to be without God,—without Christ,—without grace,—without hope,—and without heaven. It is to be in the road to hell. Now can you wonder that I ask the question,—Do You Pray?

II. *I ask again whether you pray, because a habit of prayer is one of the surest marks of a true Christian.*

All the children of God on earth are alike in this respect. From the moment there is any life and reality about their religion, they pray. Just as the first sign of life in an infant, when born into the world, is the act of breathing, so the first act of men and women, when they are born again, *is praying.*

This is one of the common marks of all the elect of God: "They cry unto Him day and night." (Luke xviii. 1.) The Holy Spirit, who makes them new creatures, works in them the feeling of adoption, and makes them cry, "Abba, Father." (Rom. viii. 15.) The Lord Jesus, when He quickens them, gives them a voice and a tongue, and says to them, "Be dumb no more." God has no dumb children. It is as much a part of their new nature to pray, as it is of a child to cry. They see their need of mercy and grace. They feel their emptiness and weakness. They cannot do otherwise than they do. They must pray.

I have looked carefully over the lives of God's saints in the Bible. I cannot find one of whose history much is told us, from Genesis to Revelation, who was not a man of prayer. I find it mentioned as a characteristic of the godly, that "they call on the Father," that "they call on the name of the Lord Jesus Christ." I find it recorded as a characteristic of the wicked, that "they call not upon the Lord." (1 Peter i. 17; 1 Cor. i. 2; Psalm xiv. 4.)

I have read the lives of many eminent Christians who have been on earth since the Bible days. Some of them, I see, were rich and some poor. Some were learned and some unlearned. Some of them were Episcopalians, some Presbyterians, some Baptists, some Independents, some Wesleyans. Some were Calvinists, and some Arminians. Some have loved to use a liturgy, and some to use none. But one thing, I see, they all had in common. They have all been *men of prayer*.

I study the reports of missionary societies in our own times. I see with joy that heathen men and women are receiving the Gospel in various parts of the globe. There are conversions in Africa, in New Zealand, in Hindostan, in America. The people converted are naturally unlike one another in every respect. But one striking thing I observe at all the missionary stations. The converted people *always pray*.

Reader, I do not deny that a man may pray without heart, and without sincerity. I do not for a moment pretend to say, that the mere fact of a person praying proves everything about his soul. As in every other part of religion, so also in this, there is plenty of deception and hypocrisy.

But this I do say,—that not praying is a clear proof

that a man is not yet a true Christian. He cannot really feel his sins. He cannot love God. He cannot feel himself a debtor to Christ. He cannot long after holiness. He cannot desire heaven. He has yet to be born again. He has yet to be made a new creature. He may boast confidently of election, grace, faith, hope, and knowledge, and deceive ignorant people. But you may rest assured it is all vain talk, *if he does not pray.*

And I say furthermore, that of all the evidences of real work of the Spirit, a habit of hearty private prayer is one of the most satisfactory that can be named. A man may preach from false motives. A man may write books, and make fine speeches, and seem diligent in good works, and yet be a Judas Iscariot. But a man seldom goes into his closet, and pours out his soul before God in secret, unless he is in earnest. The Lord Himself has set His stamp on prayer as the best proof of a true conversion. When He sent Ananias to Saul in Damascus, He gave him no other evidence of his change of heart than this, —"*Behold, he prayeth.*" (Acts ix. 11.)

I know that much may go on in a man's mind before he is brought to pray. He may have many convictions, desires, wishes, feelings, intentions, resolutions, hopes, and fears. But all these things are very uncertain evidences. They are to be found in ungodly people, and often come to nothing. In

many a case they are not more lasting than the
morning cloud, and the dew that passes away. A
real hearty prayer, flowing from a broken and contrite spirit, is worth all these things put together.

I know that the elect of God are chosen to salvation
from all eternity. I know that the Holy Spirit, who
calls them in due time, in many instances leads them
by very slow degrees to acquaintance with Christ.
But the eye of man can only judge by what it sees.
I cannot call any one justified until he believes. I
dare not say that any one believes until he prays.
I cannot understand a dumb faith. The first act of
faith will be to speak to God. Faith is to the soul
what life is to the body. Prayer is to faith what
breath is to life. How a man can live and not breathe
is past my comprehension, and how a man can believe
and not pray is past my comprehension too.

Reader, never be surprised if you hear ministers
of the Gospel dwelling much on the importance of
prayer. This is the point we want to bring you to,
—we want to know that you pray. Your views of
doctrine may be correct. Your love of Protestantism may be warm and unmistakable. But still this
may be nothing more than head knowledge and party
spirit. We want to know whether you are actually
acquainted with the throne of grace, and whether
you can speak to God as well as speak *about* God.

Reader, do you wish to find out whether you are a

true Christian? Then rest assured that my question is one of the very first importance —Do You Pray?

III. *I ask whether you pray, because there is no duty in religion so neglected as private prayer.*

We live in days of abounding religious profession. There are more places of public worship now than there ever were before. There are more persons attending them than there ever have been since England was a nation. And yet in spite of all this public religion, I believe there is a vast neglect of private prayer.

I should not have said so a few years ago. I once thought in my ignorance that most people said their prayers, and many people prayed. I have lived to think differently. I have come to the conclusion that the great majority of professing Christians do not pray at all.

I know this sounds very shocking, and will startle many. But I am satisfied that prayer is just one of those things which is thought a "matter of course," and like many matters of course is shamefully neglected. It is "everybody's business," and as it often happens in such cases, is a business carried on by very few. It is one of those private transactions between God and our souls which no eye sees, and therefore one which there is every temptation to pass over and leave undone.

I believe that thousands *never say a word of prayer at all*. They eat. They drink. They sleep. They rise. They go forth to their labour. They return to their homes. They breathe God's air. They see God's sun. They walk on God's earth. They enjoy God's mercies. They have dying bodies. They have judgment and eternity before them. But they *never speak to God*. They live like the beasts that perish. They behave like creatures without souls. They have not a word to say to Him in whose hands are their life, and breath, and all things, and from whose mouth they must one day receive their everlasting sentence. How dreadful this seems! But if the secrets of men were only known, how common!

I believe there are tens of thousands *whose prayers are nothing but a mere form*,—a set of words repeated by rote, without a thought about their meaning. Some say over a few hasty sentences picked up in the nursery when they were children. Some content themselves with repeating the Belief, forgetting that there is not a request in it. Some add the Lord's Prayer, but without the slightest desire that its solemn petitions may be granted. Some among the poor, even at this day, repeat the old popish lines:—

> "Matthew, Mark, Luke, and John,
> "Bless the bed that I lie on."

Many, even of those who use good forms, mutter their prayers over after they have got into bed; or scramble over them while they wash or dress in the morning. Men may think what they please, but they may depend that in the sight of God *this is not praying*. Words said without heart are as utterly useless to our souls as the drum-beating of the poor heathen before their idols. Where there is *no heart*, there may be lip-work and tongue-work, but there is nothing that God listens to.—there is *no prayer*. Saul, I have no doubt, said many a long prayer before the Lord met him on the way to Damascus. But it was not till his heart was broken that the Lord said, "He prayeth."

Reader, does this surprise you? Listen to me and I will show you that I am not speaking as I do without reason. Do you think that my assertions are extravagant and unwarrantable? Give me your attention, and I will soon show you that I am only telling you the truth.

Have you forgotten that it is *not natural* to any one to pray? The carnal mind is enmity against God. The desire of man's heart is to get far away from God, and have nothing to do with Him. His feeling toward Him is not love but fear. Why then should a man pray when he has no real sense of sin, no real feeling of spiritual wants,—no thorough belief in unseen things.—no desire after holiness and heaven? Of all these things the vast majority of men know and feel nothing. The multitude walk in the broad way. I cannot forget this. Therefore I say boldly, I believe that few pray.

Have you forgotten that it is *not fashionable* to pray? It is just one of the things that many would be rather ashamed to own. There are hundreds who would sooner storm a breach, or lead a forlorn hope, than confess publicly that they make a habit of prayer. There are thousands who, if obliged by chance to sleep in the same room with a stranger, would lie down in bed without a prayer. To ride well, to shoot well, to dress well, to go to balls, and concerts, and theatres, to be thought clever and agreeable, — all this is fashionable, but not to pray. I cannot forget this. I cannot think a habit is common which so many seem ashamed to own. I believe that few pray.

Have you forgotten *the lives that many live?* Can we really suppose that people are praying against sin night and day, when we see them plunging right into it? Can we suppose they pray against the world, when they are entirely absorbed and taken up with its pursuits? Can we think they really ask God for grace to serve Him, when they do not show the slightest desire to serve Him at all? Oh, no! It is plain as daylight that the great majority of men either ask nothing of

God, or *do not mean what they say* when they do ask, — which is just the same thing. Praying and sinning will never live together in the same heart. Prayer will consume sin, or sin will choke prayer. I cannot forget this. I look at men's lives. I believe that few pray.

Have you forgotten *the deaths that many die?* How many, when they draw near death, seem entirely strangers to God. Not only are they sadly ignorant of His Gospel, but sadly wanting in the power of speaking to Him. There is a terrible awkwardness, and shyness, and newness, and rawness, in their endeavours to approach Him. They seem to be taking up a fresh thing. They appear as if they wanted an introduction to God, and as if they had never talked with Him before. I remember having heard of a lady who was anxious to have a minister to visit her in her last illness. She desired that he would pray with her. He asked her what he should pray for. She did not know and could not tell. She was utterly unable to name any one thing which she wished him to ask God for her soul. All she seemed to want was the form of a minister's prayers. I can quite understand this. Deathbeds are great revealers of secrets. I cannot forget what I have seen of sick and dying people. This also leads me to believe that few pray.

IV. *I ask whether you pray, because prayer is that act in religion to which there is the greatest encouragement.*

There is everything on God's part to make prayer easy, if men will only attempt it. All things are ready on His side. Every objection is anticipated. Every difficulty is provided for. The crooked places are made straight, and the rough places are made smooth. There is no excuse left for the prayerless man.

There is *a way* by which any man, however sinful and unworthy, may draw near to God the Father. Jesus Christ has opened that way by the sacrifice He made for us upon the cross. The holiness and justice of God need not frighten sinners and keep them back. Only let them cry to God in the name of Jesus,—only let them plead the atoning blood of Jesus,—and they shall find God upon a throne of grace, willing and ready to hear. The name of Jesus is a never-failing passport to our prayers. In that name a man may draw near to God with boldness, and ask with confidence. God has engaged to hear him. Reader, think of this. Is not this encouragement?

There is *an Advocate* and Intercessor always waiting to present the prayers of those who will employ Him. That Advocate is Jesus Christ. He mingles our prayers with the incense of His own almighty intercession. So mingled they go up as a sweet savour before the throne of God. Poor as they are in themselves, they are mighty and powerful in the hand of our High Priest and elder Brother. The bank-note without a signature at the bottom, is nothing but a worthless piece of paper. The stroke of a pen confers on it all its value. The prayer of a poor child of Adam is a feeble thing in itself, but once endorsed by the hand of the Lord Jesus, it availeth much. There was an officer in the city of Rome who was appointed to have his doors always open, in order to receive any Roman citizen who applied to him for help. Just so the ear of the Lord Jesus is ever open to the cry of all who want mercy and grace. It is His office to help them. Their prayer is His delight. Reader, think of this. Is not this encouragement?

There is *the Holy Spirit* ever ready to help our infirmities in prayer. It is one part of His special office to assist us in our endeavours to speak with God. We need not be cast down and distressed by the fear of not knowing what to say. The Spirit will give us words if we will only seek His aid. He will supply us with "Thoughts that breathe and words that burn." The prayers of the Lord's people are the inspiration of the Lord's Spirit,—the work of the Holy Ghost who dwells within them as the Spirit of grace and supplications. Surely the Lord's people may well hope to be heard. It is not they merely that pray, but the Holy Ghost pleading in them. Reader, think of this. Is not this encouragement?

There are exceeding great and precious *promises* to those who pray. What did the Lord Jesus mean when He spoke such words as these, "Ask, and it shall be given you; seek, and ye shall find; knock, and it shall be opened unto you: for every one that asketh receiveth; and he that seeketh findeth; and to him that knocketh it shall be opened." (Matt. vii. 7, 8.) "All things, whatsoever ye shall ask in prayer, believing, ye shall receive." (Matt. xxi. 22.) "Whatsoever ye shall ask in my name, that will I do, that the Father may be glorified in the Son. If ye shall ask anything in my name I will do it." (John xiv. 13, 14.) What did the Lord mean when He spoke the parables of the friend at midnight and the importunate widow? (Luke xi. 5, xviii. 1.) Reader, think over these passages. If this is not encouragement to pray, words have no meaning at all.

There are wonderful *examples* in Scripture of the power of prayer. Nothing seems to be too great, too hard, or too difficult for prayer to do. It has obtained things that seemed impossible, and out of reach. It has won victories over fire, air, earth, and water. Prayer opened the Red Sea. Prayer brought water from the rock and bread from heaven. Prayer made the sun stand still. Prayer brought fire from the sky on Elijah's sacrifice. Prayer turned the counsel of Ahithophel into foolishness. Prayer overthrew the

army of Sennacherib. Well might Mary Queen of
Scots say, "I fear John Knox's prayers more than
an army of ten thousand men." Prayer has healed
the sick. Prayer has raised the dead. Prayer has
procured the conversion of souls. "The child of
many prayers," said an old Christian to Augustine's
mother, "shall never perish." Prayer, pains, and
faith can do anything. Nothing seems impossible
when a man has the spirit of adoption. "Let me
alone," is the remarkable saying of God to Moses,
when Moses was about to intercede for the children
of Israel. (Exod. xxxii. 10) The Chaldee version
has it, "leave off praying." So long as Abraham
asked mercy for Sodom, the Lord went on giving.
He never ceased to give till Abraham ceased to pray.
Reader, think of this. Is not this encouragement?

What more can a man want to lead him to take
any step in religion, than the things I have just told
him about prayer? What more could be done to
make the path to the mercy-seat easy, and to remove
all occasions of stumbling from the sinner's way?
Surely if the devils in hell had such a door set open
before them, they would leap for gladness, and make
the very pit ring with joy.

But where will the man hide his head at last who
neglects such glorious encouragements? What can
be possibly said for the man who after all dies without prayer? Surely, reader, I may well feel anxious

that you should not be that man. Surely I may well
ask,—Do You Pray?

V. *I ask whether you pray, because diligence in prayer
is the secret of eminent holiness.*

Without controversy there is a vast difference
among true Christians. There is an immense interval
between the foremost and the hindermost in the army
of God.

They are all fighting the same good fight;—but
how much more valiantly some fight than others!
They are all doing the Lord's work;—but how much
more some do than others! They are all light in the
Lord!—but now much more brightly some shine
than others! They are all running the same race;
—but how much faster some get on than others!
They all love the same Lord and Saviour;—but how
much more some love Him than others! I ask any
true Christian whether this is not the case. Are not
these things so?

There are some of the Lord's people who seem
never able to get on from the time of their conversion.
They are born again, but they remain babes all their
lives. They are learners in Christ's school, but they
never seem to get beyond A B C, and the lowest
form. They have got inside the fold, but there they
lie down and get no further. Year after year you
see in them the same old besetting sins. You hear

from them the same old experience. You remark in them the same want of spiritual appetite,—the same squeamishness about anything but the milk of the Word, and the same dislike to strong meat,—the same childishness,—the same feebleness,—the same littleness of mind,—the same narrowness of heart,— the same want of interest in anything beyond their own little circle, which you remarked ten years ago. They are pilgrims indeed, but pilgrims like the Gibeonites of old,—their bread is always dry and mouldy, their shoes always old and clouted, and their garments always rent and torn. I say this with sorrow and grief. But I ask any real Christian, Is it not true?

There are others of the Lord's people who seem to be *always getting on*. They grow like the grass after rain. They increase like Israel in Egypt. They press on like Gideon, though sometimes faint yet always pursuing. They are ever adding grace to grace, and faith to faith, and strength to strength. Every time you meet them their hearts seem larger, and their spiritual stature bigger, taller, and stronger. Every year they appear to see more, and know more, and believe more, and feel more in their religion. They not only have good works to prove the reality of their faith, but they are *zealous* of them. They not only do well, but they are *unwearied* in well doing. They attempt great things, and they do great things.

When they fail they try again, and when they fall they are soon up again. And all this time they think themselves poor unprofitable servants, and fancy they do nothing at all. These are they who make religion lovely and beautiful in the eyes of all. They wrest praise even from the unconverted, and win golden opinions even from the selfish men of the world. These are they whom it does one good to see, to be with, and to hear. When you meet them, you could believe that, like Moses, they had just come out from the presence of God. When you part with them you feel warmed by their company, as if your soul had been near a fire. I know such people are rare. I only ask, Is it not so?

Now how can we account for the difference which I have just described? What is the reason that some believers are so much brighter and holier than others? I believe the difference in nineteen cases out of twenty, arises from different habits about private prayer. I believe that those who are not eminently holy pray *little*, and those who are eminently holy pray *much*.

I dare say this opinion will startle some readers. I have little doubt that many look on eminent holiness as a kind of special gift, which none but a few must pretend to aim at. They admire it at a distance in books. They think it beautiful when they see an example near themselves. But as to its being a thing within the reach of any but a very few, such a notion never seems to enter their minds. In short, they consider it a kind of monopoly granted to a few favoured believers, but certainly not to all.

Now I believe that this is a most dangerous mistake. I believe that spiritual as well as natural greatness depends far more on the use of means within everybody's reach than on any thing else. Of course I do not say we have a right to expect a miraculous grant of intellectual gifts. But this I do say, than when a man is once converted to God, whether he shall be eminently holy or not, depends chiefly on his own diligence in the use of God's appointed means. And I assert confidently that the principal means by which most believers have become great in the Church of Christ, is the habit of *diligent private prayer*.

Look through the lives of the brightest and best of God's servants, whether in the Bible or not. See what is written of Moses, and David, and Daniel, and Paul. Mark what is recorded of Luther and Bradford, the Reformers. Observe what is related of the private devotions of Whitefield, and Cecil, and Venn, and Bickersteth, and M'Cheyne. Tell me of one of all the goodly fellowship of saints and martyrs, who has not had this mark most prominently,—he was *a man of prayer*. Oh, reader, depend upon it, prayer is power!

Prayer obtains fresh and continued out-pourings of the Spirit. He alone begins the work of grace in a man's heart. He alone can carry it forward and make it prosper. But the good Spirit loves to be entreated. And those who ask most, will always have most of His influence.

Prayer is the surest remedy against the devil and besetting sins. That sin will never stand firm which is heartily prayed against. That devil will never long keep dominion over us which we beseech the Lord to cast forth. But then we must spread out all our case before our heavenly Physician if He is to give us daily relief. We must drag our in-dwelling devils to the feet of Christ, and cry to Him to send them back to the pit.

Reader, do you wish to grow in grace and be a very holy Christian? Be very sure, if you wish it, you could not have a more important question than this,—Do You Pray?

VI. *I ask whether you pray, because neglect of prayer is one great cause of backsliding.*

There is such a thing as going back in religion after making a good profession. Men may run well for a season, like the Galatians, and then turn aside after false teachers. Men may profess loudly while their feelings are warm, as Peter did, and then in the hour of trial deny their Lord. Men may lose their first love, as the Ephesians did. Men may cool down in their zeal to do good, like Mark, the companion of Paul. Men may follow an apostle for a season, and then like Demas, go back to the world. All these things men may do.

It is a miserable thing to be a backslider. Of all unhappy things that can befall a man, I suppose it is the worst. A stranded ship, a broken-winged eagle, a garden overrun with weeds, a harp without strings, a church in ruins,—all these are sad sights, but a backslider is a sadder sight still. That true grace shall never be extinguished, and true union with Christ never be broken off, I feel no doubt. But I do believe that a man may fall away so far that he shall lose sight of his own grace, and despair of his own salvation. And if this is not hell, it is certainly the next thing to it. A wounded conscience, a mind sick of itself, a memory full of self-reproach, a heart pierced through with the Lord's arrows, a spirit broken with a load of inward accusation,—all this is *a taste of hell*. It is a hell on earth. Truly that saying of the wise man is solemn and weighty, "The backslider in heart shall be filled with his own ways." (Prov. xiv. 14.)

Now what is the cause of most backslidings? I believe as a general rule, one of the chief causes is neglect of private prayer. Of course the secret history of falls will not be known till the last day. I can only give my opinion as a minister of Christ, and a student of the heart. That opinion is, I repeat distinctly, that backsliding generally first begins with *neglect of private prayer*.

Bibles read without prayer,—sermons heard without prayer,—marriages contracted without prayer,—journeys undertaken without prayer,—residences chosen without prayer,—friendships formed without prayer,—the daily act of private prayer itself hurried over, or gone through without heart,—these are the kind of downward steps by which many a Christian descends to a condition of spiritual palsy, or reaches the point where God allows him to have a tremendous fall.

This is the process which form the lingering Lots, the unstable Samsons, the wife idolizing Solomons, the inconsistent Asas, the pliable Jehoshaphats, the over-careful Marthas,—of whom so many are to be found in the Church of Christ. Often the simple history of such cases is this,—they became *careless about private prayer*.

Reader, you may be very sure men fall in private long before they fall in public. They are backsliders on their knees long before they backslide openly in the eyes of the world. Like Peter, they first disregard the Lord's warning to watch and pray, and then, like Peter, their strength is gone, and in the hour of temptation they deny their Lord.

The world takes notice of their fall, and scoffs loudly. But the world knows nothing of the real reason. The heathen succeeded in making the old Christian, Origen, offer incense to an idol, by threatening him with a punishment worse than death. They then triumphed greatly at the sight of his cowardice and apostasy. But the heathen did not know the fact, which Origen himself tells us, that on that very morning he had left his bed-chamber hastily, and without finishing his usual prayers.

Reader, if you are a Christian indeed, I trust you will never be a backslider. But if you do not wish to be a backsliding Christian, remember the question I ask you,—Do You Pray?

VII. *I ask, lastly, whether you pray, because prayer is one of the best receipts for happiness and contentment.*

We live in a world where sorrow abounds. This has always been its state since sin came in. There cannot be sin without sorrow. And till sin is driven out from the world, it is vain for any one to suppose he can escape sorrow.

Some without doubt have a larger cup of sorrow to drink than others. But few are to be found who live long without sorrows or care of some sort or another. Our bodies, our property, our families, our children, our relations, our servants, our friends, our neighbours, our worldly callings,—each and all of these are fountains of care. Sicknesses, deaths, losses, disappointments, partings, separations, ingratitude, slander,—all these are common things. We cannot get through life without them. Some day or other they find us out. The greater are our affections, the deeper are our afflictions, and the more we love the more we have to weep.

And what is the best receipt for cheerfulness in such a world as this? How shall we get through this valley of tears with least pain? I know no better receipt than the habit of *taking everything to God in prayer*.

This is the plain advice that the Bible gives, both in the Old Testament and in the New. What says the Psalmist? "Call upon Me in the day of trouble and I will deliver thee, and thou shalt glorify Me." (Psalm l. 15.) "Cast thy burden upon the Lord, and He shall sustain thee: He shall never suffer the righteous to be moved." (Psalm lv. 22.) What says the apostle Paul? "Be careful for nothing; but in everything by prayer and supplication with thanksgiving let your requests be made known unto God. And the peace of God, which passeth all understanding, shall keep your hearts and minds through Christ Jesus." (Phil. iv. 6, 7.) What says the apostle James? "Is any afflicted among you? let him pray."

This was the practice of all the saints whose history

we have recorded in the Scriptures. This is what Jacob did when he feared his brother Esau. This is what Moses did when the people were ready to stone him in the wilderness. This is what Joshua did when Israel was defeated before Ai. This is what David did when he was in danger at Keilah. This is what Hezekiah did when he received the letter from Sennacherib. This is what the Church did when Peter was put in prison. This is what Paul did when he was cast into the dungeon at Philippi.

The only way to be really happy in such a world as this, is to be ever casting all our cares on God. It is the trying to carry their own burdens which so often makes believers sad. If they will only tell their troubles to God, He will enable them to bear them as easily as Samson did the gates of Gaza. If they are resolved to keep them to themselves, they will find one day that the very grasshopper is a burden.

There is a friend ever waiting to help us if we will only unbosom to Him our sorrow, a friend who pitied the poor, and sick, and sorrowful, when He was upon earth,—a friend who knows the heart of man, for He lived thirty-three years as a man amongst us,—a friend who can weep with the weepers, for He was a man of sorrows and acquainted with grief,—a friend who is able to help us, for there never was earthly pain He could not cure. That friend is Jesus

Christ. The way to be happy is to be always opening our hearts to Him. Oh, that we were all like
that poor Christian negro who only answered, when
threatened and punished, "I *must tell the Lord.*"

Jesus can make those happy who trust Him and
call on Him, whatever be their outward condition.
He can give them peace of heart in a prison,—contentment in the midst of poverty,—comfort in the
midst of bereavements,—joy on the brink of the
grave. There is a mighty fulness in Him for all
His believing members,—a fulness that is ready to
be poured out on every one that will ask in prayer.
Oh, that men would understand that happiness does
not depend on outward circumstances, but on the
state of the heart.

Prayer can lighten crosses for us however heavy.
It can bring down to our side One who will help us
to bear them. Prayer can open a door for us when
our way seems hedged up. It can bring down One
who will say, "This is the way, walk in it." Prayer
can let in a ray of hope when all our earthly prospects seem darkened. It can bring down One who
will say, "I will never leave thee nor forsake thee."
Prayer can obtain relief for us when those we love
most are taken away, and the world feels empty.
It can bring down One who can fill the gap in our
hearts with Himself, and say to the waves within,
"Peace: be still." Oh, that men were not so like

Hagar in the wilderness, blind to the well of living waters close beside them!

Reader, I want you to be happy. I know I cannot ask you a more useful question than this,—Do YOU PRAY?

And now, reader, it is high time for me to bring this tract to an end. I trust I have brought before you things that will be seriously considered. I heartily pray God that this consideration may be blessed to your soul.

1. Let me speak a parting word *to those who do not pray*. I dare not suppose that all who read these pages will be praying people. If you are a prayerless person, suffer me to speak to you this day on God's behalf.

Prayerless reader, I can only warn you, but I do warn you most solemnly. I warn you that you are in a position of fearful danger. If you die in your present state you are a lost soul. You will only rise again to be eternally miserable. I warn you that of all professing Christians you are most utterly without excuse. There is not a single good reason that you can show for living without prayer.

It is useless to say you *know not how* to pray. Prayer is the simplest act in all religion. It is simply speaking to God. It needs neither learning, nor wisdom, nor book-knowledge to begin it. It needs nothing but heart and will. The weakest infant can cry when he is hungry. The poorest beggar can hold out his hand for an alms, and does not wait to find fine words. The most ignorant man will find something to say to God, if he has only a mind.

It is useless to say you have *no convenient place* to pray in. Any man can find a place private enough if he is disposed. Our Lord prayed on a mountain: Peter on the house-top: Isaac in the field: Nathanael under the fig tree: Jonah in the whale's belly. Any place may become a closet, an oratory, and a Bethel, and be to us the presence of God.

It is useless to say *you have no time*. There is plenty of time, if men will only employ it. Time may be short, but time is always long enough for prayer. Daniel had all the affairs of a kingdom on his hands, and yet he prayed three times a day. David was ruler over a mighty nation, and yet he says, "Evening and morning and at noon will I pray." (Psalm lv. 17.) When time is really wanted, time can always be found.

It is useless to say you *cannot pray till you have faith and a new heart*, and that you must sit still and wait for them. This is to add sin to sin. It is bad enough to be unconverted and going to hell. It is even worse to say, "I know it, but will not cry for mercy." This is a kind of argument for which there is no warrant in Scripture. "Call ye upon the Lord," saith Isaiah, "while He is near." (Isai. lv. 6.) "Take with you words and come unto the Lord," says Hosea. (Hosea xiv. 1.) "Repent and pray," says Peter to Simon Magus. (Acts viii. 22.) If you want faith and a new heart, go and cry to the Lord for them. This very attempt to pray has often been the quickening of a dead soul. Alas, there is no devil so dangerous as a dumb devil!

Oh, prayerless reader! who and what are you that you will not ask anything of God? Have you made a covenant with death and hell? Are you at peace with the worm and the fire? Have you no sins to be pardoned? Have you no fear of eternal torment? Have you no desire after heaven? Oh, that you would awake from your present folly! Oh, that you would consider your latter end! Oh, that you would arise and call upon God! Alas, there is a day coming when many shall pray loudly, "Lord, Lord, open to us!" but all too late;—when many shall cry to the rocks to fall on them, and to the hills to cover them, who would never cry to God. Reader, in all affection I warn you. Beware lest this be the end of your soul. Salvation is very near you. Do not lose heaven for want of asking.

2. Let me speak, in the next place, *to those who have real desires for salvation*, but know not what steps to take or where to begin. I cannot but hope that

some readers may be in this state of mind, and if there be but one such I must offer him encouragement and advice.

In every journey there must be a first step. There must be a change from sitting still to moving forward. The journeyings of Israel from Egypt to Canaan were long and wearisome. Forty years passed away before they crossed Jordan. Yet there was some one who moved first when they marched from Rameses to Succoth. When does a man really take his first step in coming out from sin and the world? He does it in the day when he first prays with his heart.

In every building the first stone must be laid, and the first blow must be struck. The ark was 120 years in building. Yet there was a day when Noah laid his axe to the first tree he cut down to form it. The temple of Solomon was a glorious building. But there was a day when the first huge stone was laid at the foot of Mount Moriah. When does the building of the Spirit really begin to appear in a man's heart? It begins, so far as we can judge, when he first pours out his heart to God in prayer.

Reader, if you desire salvation, and want to know what to do, I advise you to go this very day to the Lord Jesus Christ, in the first private place you can find, and entreat Him in prayer to save your soul.

Tell Him that you have heard that He receives sinners, and has said, " Him that cometh unto me I will in no wise cast out." Tell Him that you are a poor vile sinner, and that you come to Him on the faith of His own invitation. Tell Him you put yourself wholly and entirely in His hands —that you feel vile and helpless, and hopeless in yourself — and that except He saves you, you have no hope to be saved at all. Beseech Him to deliver you from the guilt, the power, and the consequences of sin. Beseech Him to pardon you and wash you in His own blood. Beseech Him to give you a new heart, and plant the Holy Spirit in your soul. Beseech Him to give you grace, and faith, and will, and power to be His disciple and servant from this day for ever. Oh, reader! go this very day, and tell these things to the Lord Jesus Christ, if you really are in earnest about your soul.

Tell Him in your own way, and your own words. If a doctor came to see you when sick, you could tell him where you felt pain. If your soul feels its disease indeed, you can surely find something to tell Christ.

Doubt not His willingness to save you, because you are a sinner. It is Christ's office to save sinners. He says Himself, "I came not to call the righteous, but sinners to repentance." (Luke v. 32.)

Wait not because you feel unworthy. Wait for nothing. Wait for nobody. Waiting comes from the devil. Just as you are, go to Christ. The worse you are, the more need you have to apply to Him. You will never mend yourself by staying away.

Fear not, because your prayer is stammering,— your words feeble, and your language poor. Jesus can understand you. Just as a mother understands the first babblings of her infant, so does the blessed Saviour understand sinners. He can read a sigh, and see a meaning in a groan.

Despair not because you do not get an answer immediately. While you are speaking, Jesus is listening. If He delays an answer, it is only for wise reasons, and to try if you are in earnest. Pray on, and the answer will surely come. Though it tarry, wait for it. It will surely come at last.

Oh, reader! if you have any desire to be saved, remember the advice I have given you this day. Act upon it honestly and heartily, and you shall be saved.

3. Let me speak, lastly, *to those who do pray.* I trust that some who read this book know well what prayer is, and have the spirit of adoption. To all such, I offer a few words of brotherly counsel and exhortation. The incense offered in the tabernacle was ordered to be made in a particular way. Not every kind of incense would do. Let us remember this, and be careful about the matter and manner of our prayers.

Brethren who pray, if I know anything of a Christian's heart, you are often sick of your own prayers. You never enter into the Apostle's words, "When I would do good, evil is present with me," so thoroughly as you sometimes do upon your knees. You can understand David's words, "I hate vain thoughts." You can sympathize with that poor converted Hottentot, who was overheard praying, "Lord deliver me from all my enemies, and above all from that bad man myself!" There are few children of God, who do not often find the season of prayer a season of conflict. The devil has special wrath against us, when he sees us on our knees. Yet I believe that prayers which cost us no trouble, should be regarded with great suspicion. I believe we are very poor judges of the goodness of our prayers, and that the prayer which pleases us *least*, often pleases God *most*. Suffer me then, as a companion in the Christian warfare, to offer you a few words of exhortation. One thing, at least, we all feel: we must pray. We cannot give it up. We must go on.

I commend then to your attention, the importance of *reverence and humility* in prayer. Let us never forget what we are, and what a solemn thing it is to speak with God. Let us beware of rushing into His presence with carelessness and levity. Let us say to ourselves, "I am on holy ground. This is no other than the gate of heaven. If I do not mean what I say, I am trifling with God. If I regard iniquity in my heart, the Lord will not hear me." Let us keep in mind the words of Solomon, "Be not rash with thy mouth, and let not thine heart be hasty to utter anything before God; for God is in heaven, and thou on earth." (Eccles. v. 2.) When Abraham spoke to God, he said, "I am dust and ashes." When Job, he said, "I am vile." Let us do likewise.

I commend to you, in the next place, the importance of praying *spiritually*. I mean by that, that we should labour always to have the direct help of the Spirit in our prayers, and beware above all things of formality. There is nothing so spiritual, but that it may become a form, and this is specially true of private prayer. We may insensibly get into the habit of using the fittest possible words, and offering the most Scriptural petitions, and yet do it all by rote without feeling it, and walk daily round an old beaten path, like a horse in a mill. I desire to touch this point with caution and delicacy. I know that there are certain great things we daily want, and that there is nothing necessarily formal in asking for these things in the same words. The world, the devil, and our hearts, are daily the same. Of necessity we must daily go over old ground. But this I say, we must be very careful on this point. If the skeleton and outline of our prayers be by habit almost a form, let us strive that the clothing and filling up of our prayers, be as far as possible of the

Spirit. As to praying out of a book, it is a habit I
cannot praise. If we can tell our doctors the state
of our bodies without a book, we ought to be able
to tell the state of our souls to God. I have no
objection to a man using crutches, when he is first
recovering from a broken limb. It is better to use
crutches than not to walk at all. But if I saw him
all his life on crutches, I should not think it matter
for congratulation. I should like to see him strong
enough to throw his crutches away.

I commend to you, in the next place, the importance of making prayer *a regular business of life*. I
might say something of the value of regular times in
the day for prayer. God is a God of order. The
hours for morning and evening sacrifice in the Jewish
temple were not fixed as they were without a meaning. Disorder is eminently one of the fruits of sin.
But I would not bring any under bondage. This
only I say, that it is essential to your soul's health to
make prayer a part of the business of every twenty-
four hours in your life. Just as you allot time to
eating, sleeping, and business, so also allot time to
prayer. Choose your own hours and seasons. At
the very least speak with God in the morning, before
you speak with the world; and speak with God at
night, after you have done with the world. But
settle it down in your minds, that prayer is one of
the great things of every day. Do not drive it into

a corner. Do not give it the scraps and leavings and parings of your day. Whatever else you make a business of, make a business of prayer.

I commend to you, in the next place, the importance of *perseverance* in prayer. Once having begun the habit, never give it up. Your heart will sometimes say, "You have had family prayers; what mighty harm if you leave private prayer undone?" Your body will sometimes say, "You are unwell, or sleepy, or weary; you need not pray." Your mind will sometimes say, "You have important business to attend to to-day; cut short your prayers." Look on all such suggestions as coming direct from the devil. They are all as good as saying, "Neglect your soul." I do not maintain that prayers should always be of the same length;—but I do say, let no excuse make you give up prayer. It is not for nothing that Paul said, "Continue in prayer," and "Pray without ceasing." He did not mean that men should be always on their knees, as an old sect, called the Euchitæ, supposed. But he did mean that our prayers should be like the continual burnt offering, —a thing steadily persevered in every day ;—that it should be like seed-time and harvest, and summer and winter,—a thing that should unceasingly come round at regular seasons ;—that it should be like the fire on the altar, not always consuming sacrifices, but never completely going out. Never forget that you may tie together morning and evening devotions, by an endless chain of short ejaculatory prayers throughout the day. Even in company, or business, or in the very streets, you may be silently sending up little winged messengers to God, as Nehemiah did in the very presence of Artaxerxes. And never think that time is wasted which is given to God. A nation does not become poorer because it loses one year of working days in seven, by keeping the Sabbath. A Christian never finds he is a loser in the long run, by persevering in prayer.

I commend to you, in the next place, the importance of *earnestness* in prayer. It is not necessary that a man should shout, or scream, or be very loud, in order to prove that he is in earnest. But it is desirable that we should be hearty, and fervent, and warm, and ask as if we were really interested in what we were doing. It is the "effectual fervent" prayer that "availeth much," and not the cold, sleepy, lazy, listless one. This is the lesson that is taught us by the expressions used in Scripture about prayer. It is called "crying, knocking, wrestling, labouring, striving." This is the lesson taught us by Scripture examples. Jacob is one. He said to the angel at Penuel, "I will not let thee go, except thou bless me." (Gen. xxii. 26.) Daniel is another. Hear how he pleadeth with God: "O Lord, hear; O Lord, forgive; O Lord, hearken and do, defer not, for thine own sake, O my God." (Dan. ix. 19.) Our Lord Jesus Christ is another. It is written of Him, "In the days of His flesh he offered up prayer and supplication, with strong crying and tears." (Heb. v. 7.) Alas, how unlike is this to many of our supplications! How tame and lukewarm they seem by comparison! How truly might God say to many of us, "You do not really want what you pray for!" Let us try to amend this fault. Let us knock loudly at the door of grace, like Mercy in "Pilgrim's Progress," as if we must perish unless heard. Let us settle it down in our minds, that cold prayers are a sacrifice without fire. Let us remember the story of Demosthenes, the great orator, when one came to him, and wanted him to plead his cause. He heard him without attention, while he told his story without earnestness. The man saw this, and cried out with anxiety that it was all true. "Ah!" said Demosthenes, "I believe you *now*."

I commend to you, in the next place, the importance of *praying with faith*. We should endeavour to believe that our prayers are always heard, and that if we ask things according to God's will, shall always be answered. This is the plain command of our Lord Jesus Christ: "Whatsoever things ye desire, when ye pray, believe that ye receive them, and ye shall have them." (Mark xi. 24.) Faith is to prayer what the feather is to the arrow: without it prayer will not hit the mark. We should cultivate the habit of pleading promises in our prayers. We should take with us some promise, and say, "Lord, here is thine own word pledged. Do for us as Thou hast said." This was the habit of Jacob, and Moses, and David. The 119th Psalm is full of things asked, "according to Thy word." Above all, we should cultivate the habit of expecting answers to our prayers. We should do like the merchant who sends his ships to sea. We should not be satisfied unless we see some return. Alas, there are few points on which Christians come short so much as this! The Church at Jerusalem made prayer without ceasing for Peter in prison; but when the prayer was answered, they would hardly believe it. (Acts xii. 15.) It is a solemn saying of old Traill's, "There is no surer mark of trifling in prayer, than when men are careless what they get by prayer."

I commend to you, in the next place, the importance of *boldness* in prayer. There is an unseemly familiarity in some men's prayers which I cannot praise. But there is such a thing as a holy boldness, which is exceedingly to be desired. I mean such boldness as that of Moses, when he pleads with God not to destroy Israel: "Wherefore," says he, "should the Egyptians speak and say, For mischief did He bring them out, to slay them in the mountains? Turn from Thy fierce anger." (Exod. xxxii.

12.) I mean such boldness as that of Joshua, when the children of Israel were defeated before Ai: "What," says he, "wilt Thou do to Thy great name?" (Josh. vii. 9.) This is the boldness for which Luther was remarkable. One who heard him praying said, " What a spirit,—what a confidence was in his very expressions! With such a reverence he sued, as one begging of God, and yet with such hope and assurance, as if he spake with a loving father or friend." This is the boldness which distinguished Bruce, a great Scotch divine of the 17th century. His prayers were said to be "like bolts shot up into heaven." Here also I fear we sadly come short. We do not sufficiently realize the believer's privileges. We do not plead as often as we might, "Lord, are we not thine own people? Is it not for Thy glory that we should be sanctified? Is it not for thine honour that Thy Gospel should increase?"

I commend to you, in the next place, the importance of *fulness* in prayer. I do not forget that our Lord warns us against the example of the Pharisees, who for pretence make long prayers; and commands us when we pray not to use vain repetitions. But I cannot forget, on the other hand, that He has given His own sanction to large and long devotions, by continuing all night in prayer to God. At all events we are not likely in this day to err on the side of praying *too much*. Might it not rather be feared,

that many believers in this generation pray *too little?*
Is not the actual amount of time that many Christians
give to prayer in the aggregate very small? I am
afraid these questions cannot be answered satisfac-
torily. I am afraid the private devotions of many
are most painfully scanty and limited,—just enough
to prove that they are alive, and no more. They
really seem to want little from God. They seem to
have little to confess, little to ask for, and little
to thank Him for. Alas, this is altogether wrong!
Nothing is more common than to hear believers
complaining that they do not get on. They tell us
that they do not grow in grace as they could desire.
Is it not rather to be suspected that many have quite
as much grace as they ask for? Is it not the true
account of many, that they have little because they
ask little?

The cause of their weakness is to be found in their
own stunted, dwarfish, clipped, contracted, hurried,
little, narrow, diminutive prayers. *They have not because they ask not.* Oh, reader! we are not straitened
in Christ, but in ourselves. The Lord says, "Open
thy mouth wide, and I will fill it." But we are like
the king of Israel, who smote on the ground thrice
and stayed, when he ought to have smitten five or
six times.

I commend to you, in the next place, the importance
of *particularity* in prayer. We ought not to be

content with great general petitions. We ought to specify our wants before the throne of grace. It should not be enough to confess we are sinners. We should name the sins of which our conscience tells us we are most guilty. It should not be enough to ask for holiness. We should name the graces in which we feel most deficient. It should not be enough to tell the Lord we are in trouble. We should describe our trouble and all its peculiarities. This is what Jacob did when he feared his brother Esau. He tells God exactly what it is that he fears. (Gen. xxxii. 11.) This is what Eliezer did, when he sought a wife for his master's son. He spreads before God precisely what he wants. (Gen. xxiv. 12.) This is what Paul did when he had a thorn in the flesh. He besought the Lord. (2 Cor. xii. 8.) This is true faith and confidence. We should believe that nothing is too small to be named before God. What should we think of the patient who told his doctor he was ill, but never went into particulars? What should we think of the wife who told her husband she was unhappy, but did not specify the cause? What should we think of the child who told his father he was in trouble, but nothing more? Oh, reader! Christ is the true Bridegroom of the soul,—the true Physician of the heart,—the real Father of all His people. Let us show that we feel this, by being unreserved in our communications with Him. Let us

hide no secrets from Him. Let us tell Him all our
hearts.

I commend to you, in the next place, the importance of *intercession* in our prayers. We are all
selfish by nature, and our selfishness is very apt to
stick to us, even when we are converted. There is
a tendency in us to think only of our own souls,—
our own spiritual conflict,—our own progress in religion, and to forget others. Against this tendency
we have all need to watch and strive, and not least
in our prayers. We should study to be of a public
spirit. We should stir ourselves up to name other
names beside our own, before the throne of grace.
We should try to bear in our hearts the whole world,
—the heathen,—the Jews,—the Roman Catholics,—
the body of true believers,—the professing Protestant
Churches,—the country in which we live,—the congregation to which we belong,—the household in
which we sojourn,—the friends and relations we are
connected with. For each and all of these, we should
plead. This is the highest charity. He loves me best
who loves me in his prayers. This is for our soul's
health. It enlarges our sympathies and expands our
hearts. This is for the benefit of the Church. The
wheels of all machinery for extending the Gospel, are
oiled by prayer. They do as much for the Lord's
cause who intercede like Moses on the mount, as they
do who fight like Joshua in the thick of the battle.

This is to be like Christ. He bears the names of His people on His breast and shoulders, as their High Priest before the Father. Oh, the privilege of being like Jesus! This is to be a true helper to ministers. If I must needs choose a congregation, give me a people that pray.

I commend to you, in the next place, the importance of *thankfulness* in prayer. I know well that asking God is one thing, and praising God is another. But I see so close a connection between prayer and praise in the Bible, that I dare not call that true prayer, in which thankfulness has no part. It is not for nothing that Paul says, " By prayer and supplication, with thanksgiving let your requests be made known unto God." (Phil. iv. 6.) "Continue in prayer, and watch in the same, with thanksgiving." (Coloss. iv. 2.) It is of mercy that we are not in hell. It is of mercy that we have the hope of heaven. It is of mercy that we live in a land of spiritual light. It is of mercy that we have been called by the Spirit, and not left to reap the fruit of our own ways. It is of mercy that we still live and have opportunities of glorifying God actively or passively. Surely, these thoughts should crowd on our minds whenever we speak with God. Surely, we should never open our lips in prayer without blessing God for that free grace by which we live, and for that lovingkindness which endureth for ever. Never was there an eminent saint who was not full of thankfulness. St. Paul hardly ever writes an epistle without beginning with thankfulness. Men like Whitefield in the last century, and Bickersteth in our own time, were ever running over with thankfulness. Oh, reader, if we would be bright and shining lights in our day, we must cherish a spirit of praise. And above all, let our prayers be thankful prayers.

I commend to you, in the last place, the importance of *watchfulness over your prayers*. Prayer is that point of all others in religion, at which you must be on your guard. Here it is that true religion begins,—here it flourishes, and here it decays. Tell me what a man's prayers are, and I will soon tell you the state of his soul. Prayer is the spiritual pulse. By this the spiritual health may always be tested. Prayer is the spiritual weather-glass. By this we may always know whether it is fair or foul with our hearts. Oh, let us keep an eye continually upon our private devotions! Here is the pith, and marrow, and back-bone of our practical Christianity. Sermons, and books, and tracts, and committee meetings, and the company of good men, are all good in their way, but they will never make up for the neglect of private prayer. Mark well the places, and society, and companions that unhinge your hearts for communion with God, and make your prayers drive heavily. *There be on your guard.* Observe narrowly what friends, and what employments leave your soul in the most spiritual frame, and most ready to speak with God. *To these cleave and stick fast.* Reader, if you will only take care of your prayers, I will engage that nothing shall go very wrong with your soul.

Reader, I offer these points for your private consideration. I do it in all humility. I know no one who needs to be reminded of them more than I do myself. But I believe them to be God's own truth, and I should like myself and all I love to feel them more.

I want the times we live in to be praying times. I want the Christians of our day to be praying Christians. I want the Church of our age to be a praying Church. My heart's desire and prayer in sending forth these pages is to promote a spirit of prayerfulness. I want those who never prayed yet, to arise and call upon God, and I want those who do pray, to see that they are not praying amiss.

And now if any one should begin to pray, or should pray more earnestly in consequence of reading this volume, I will ask him to do the writer of it one single favour, and that is, *to remember him in his prayers.*

Wheat or Chaff?

MATTHEW III. 12

*" Whose fan is in his hand, and he will throughly purge
his floor, and gather his wheat into the garner; but
he will burn up the chaff with unquenchable fire."*

You see a question at the head of this page. For
whom do you think it is meant? Is it for corn merchants and farmers only, and for none else? If you
think so you are much mistaken. It is meant for
every man, woman, and child in the world. And
among others, it is meant for you.

The question is drawn from a verse of Scripture
which is now before your eyes. The words of that
verse were spoken by John the Baptist. They are a
prophecy about our Lord Jesus Christ, and a prophecy
which has not yet been fulfilled. They are a prophecy

which we shall all see fulfilled one day, and God alone knows how soon.

Reader, I invite you this day to consider the great truths which this verse contains. I invite you to listen to me, while I unfold them and set them before you in order. Who knows but this text may prove a word in season to your soul? Who knows but my question may help to make this day the happiest day in your life?

Listen, before you begin once more your appointed path of duty. Listen, before you start once more on some round of business. Listen, before you plunge once more into some course of useless idleness and folly. Listen to one who loves your soul, and would fain help to save it, or draw it nearer to Christ. Who knows what a day may bring forth? Who can tell whether you will live to see to-morrow. Be still, and listen to me a few minutes, while I show you something out of the Word of God.

I. Let me show you in the first place, *the two great classes into which the world may be divided*.

There are only two classes of people in the world, in the sight of God, and both are mentioned in the text which begins this tract. There are those who are called *the wheat*, and there are those who are called *the chaff*.

Viewed with the eye of man, the earth contains

many different sorts of inhabitants. Viewed with the eye of God, it only contains two. Man's eye looks at the outward appearance: this is all he thinks of. The eye of God looks at the heart: this is the only part of which He takes any account. And tried by the state of their hearts, there are but two classes into which people can be divided,—either they are wheat or they are chaff.

Reader, who are the wheat in the world? Listen to me, and I will tell you.

The wheat means all men and women who are believers in the Lord Jesus Christ,—all who are led by the Holy Spirit,—all who have felt themselves sinners, and fled for refuge to the salvation offered in the Gospel,—all who love the Lord Jesus, and live to the Lord Jesus, and serve the Lord Jesus,— all who have taken Christ for their only confidence, and the Bible for their only guide, and regard sin as their deadliest enemy, and look to heaven as their only home. All such, of every church, name, nation, people, and tongue,—of every rank, station, condition, and degree,—all such are God's wheat.

Show me men of this kind anywhere, and I know what they are. I know not that they and I may agree in all particulars, but I see in them the handiwork of the King of kings, and I ask no more. I know not whence they came, and where they found their religion; but I know where they are going,

and that is enough for me. They are the children
of my Father in heaven. They are part of His
wheat.

All such, though sinful, and vile, and unworthy in
their own eyes, are the precious part of mankind.
They are the sons and daughters of God the Father.
They are the delight of God the Son. They are the
habitation of God the Spirit. The Father beholds
no iniquity in them:—they are the members of His
dear Son's body: in Him He sees them, and is well
pleased. The Lord Jesus discerns in them the fruit
of His own travail and work upon the cross, and is
well satisfied. The Holy Ghost regards them as
spiritual temples which He Himself has reared, and
rejoices over them. In a word, they are the wheat
of the earth.

Reader, who are the chaff in the world? Listen
to me once more, and I will tell you this also.

The chaff means all men and women who have no
saving faith in Christ, and no sanctification of the
Spirit, whosoever they may be. Some of them
perhaps are infidels, and some are formal Christians.
Some are sneering Sadducees, and some self-righteous
Pharisees. Some of them make a point of keeping
up a kind of Sunday religion, and others are utterly
careless of everything except their own pleasure and
the world. But all alike, who have the two great
marks already mentioned —*no faith and no sanctifica-*

tion,—all such are chaff.   From Paine and Voltaire
to the dead churchman who can think of nothing but
outward ceremonies,—from Julian and Porphyry to
the unconverted admirer of sermons in the present
day,—all, all are standing in one rank before God :
all, all are chaff.

They bring no glory to God the Father.   They
honour not the Son, and so do not honour the Father
that sent Him.   They neglect that mighty salvation,
which countless millions of angels admire.   They
disobey that Word which was graciously written for
their learning.   They listen not to the voice of Him
who condescended to leave heaven and die for their
sins.   They pay no tribute of service and affection to
Him who gave them life, and breath, and all things.
And therefore God takes no pleasure in them.   He
pities them, but He reckons them no better than
chaff.

Yes : you may have rare intellectual gifts, and
high mental attainments,—you may sway kingdoms
by your counsel, move millions by your pen, or keep
crowds in breathless attention by your tongue ; but
if you have never submitted yourself to the yoke of
Christ, and never honoured His Gospel by heartfelt
reception of it, you are nothing in His sight.   Natural gifts without grace are like a row of cyphers
without an unit before them : they look big, but they
are of no value.   The meanest insect that crawls is

a nobler being than you are. It fills its place in creation, and glorifies its Maker with all its power, and you do not. You do not honour God with heart, and will, and intellect, and members, which are all His. You invert His order and arrangement, and live as if time was of more importance than eternity, and body better than soul. You dare to neglect God's greatest gift, His own incarnate Son. You are cold about that subject which fills all heaven with hallelujahs. And so long as this is the case, you belong to the worthless part of mankind. You are the chaff of the earth.

Reader, let this thought be graven deeply in your mind, whatever else you forget in this volume. Remember there are only two sorts of people in the world. There are wheat, and there are chaff.

There are many nations in Europe. Each differs from the rest. Each has its own language, its own laws, its own peculiar customs. But God's eye divides Europe into two great parties,—the wheat and the chaff.

There are many classes in England. There are peers and commoners,—farmers and shopkeepers,— masters and servants,—rich and poor. But God's eye only takes account of two orders,—the wheat and the chaff.

There are many and various minds in every con- gregation that meets for religious worship. There are some who attend for a mere form, and some who really desire to meet Christ,—some who come there to please others, and some who come to please God, —some who bring their hearts with them, and are not soon tired, and some who leave their hearts behind them, and reckon the whole service weary work. But the eye of Jesus only sees two divisions in the congregation,—the wheat and the chaff.

There were millions of visitors to the Great Exhibition of 1851. From Europe, Asia, Africa, and America,—from North, and South, and East, and West,—crowds came together to see what skill and industry could do. Children of our first father Adam's family, who had never seen each other before, for once met face to face under one roof. But the eye of the Lord only saw two companies thronging that large palace of glass,—the wheat and the chaff.

Reader, I know well the world dislikes this way of dividing professing Christians. The world tries hard to fancy there are *three* sorts of people, and not *two*. To be very good and very strict does not suit the world : they cannot, will not be saints. To have no religion at all does not suit the world : it would not be respectable ;—" Thank God," they will say, "we are not so bad as that." But to have religion enough to be saved, and yet not go into extremes,— to be sufficiently good, and yet not be peculiar,—to have a quiet, easy-going, moderate kind of Christianity, and go comfortably to heaven after all,—this is the world's favourite idea. There is a third class, a safe middle class,—the world fancies; and in this middle class the majority of men persuade themselves they will be found.

Reader, I denounce this notion of a middle class as an immense and soul-ruining delusion. I warn you strongly not to be carried away by it. It is as vain an invention as the Pope's purgatory. It is a refuge of lies, a castle in the air, a Russian ice-palace, a vast unreality, an empty dream. This middle class is a class of Christians no where spoken of in the Bible.

There were two classes in the day of Noah's flood; those who were inside the ark, and those who were without:—two in the parable of the Gospel net; those who are called the good fish, and those who are called the bad;—two in the parable of the ten virgins; those who are described as wise, and those who are described as foolish;—two in the account of the judgment day; the sheep and the goats;—two sides of the throne; the right hand and the left;—two abodes when the last sentence has been passed; heaven and hell.

And just so there are only two classes in the visible Church on earth; those who are in the state of nature, and those who are in the state of grace,—those who are in the narrow way, and those who are in the broad,— those who have faith, and those who have not faith,—

those who have been converted, and those who have
not been converted,—those who are with Christ, and
those who are against Him,—those who gather with
Him, and those who scatter abroad,—those who are
wheat and those who are chaff. Into these two classes
the whole professing Church of Christ may be divided.
Beside these two classes there is none.

Reader, dear reader, see now what cause there is
for self-inquiry. Are you among the wheat, or among
the chaff? Neutrality is imposible. Either you are
in one class, or in the other. Which is it of the two?

You attend church perhaps. You go to the Lord's
table. You like good people. You can distinguish
between good preaching and bad. You think Popery
false, and oppose it warmly. You think Protestantism
true, and support it cordially. You subscribe to religious societies. You attend religious meetings. You
sometimes read religious books. It is well: it is very
well. It is good: it is all very good. It is more
than can be said of many. But still this is not a
straightforward answer to my question,—Are you
wheat, or are you chaff?

Have you been born again? Are you a new
creature? Have you put off the old man, and put
on the new? Have you ever felt your sins, and repented of them? Are you looking simply to Christ
for pardon and life eternal. Do you love Christ?
Do you serve Christ? Do you loathe heart-sins, and

fight against them? Do you long for perfect holiness, and follow hard after it? Have you come out from the world? Do you delight in the Bible? Do you wrestle in prayer? Do you love Christ's people? Do you try to do good to the world? Are you vile in your own eyes, and willing to take the lowest place? Are you a Christian in business, and on week days, and by your own fireside? Oh, think, think, think on these things, and then perhaps you will be better able to tell the state of your soul?

Reader, I beseech you not to turn away from my question, however unpleasant it may be. Answer it, though it may prick your conscience, and cut you to the heart. Answer it, though it may prove you in the wrong, and expose your fearful danger. Rest not, rest not, till you know how it is between you and God. Better a thousand times find out that you are in an evil case, and repent betimes, than live on in uncertainty, and be lost eternally.

Reader, remember my question.—Begin to meditate on it this very day. Are you wheat or chaff?

II. Let me show you, in the second place, *the time when the two great classes of mankind shall be separated.*

The text at the beginning of this tract foretells a separation. It says that Christ shall one day do to His professing Church what the farmer does to his corn. He shall winnow and sift it. He "shall throughly purge His floor." And then the wheat and the chaff shall be divided.

There is no separation yet. Good and bad are now all mingled together in the visible Church of Christ. Believers and unbelievers,—converted and unconverted,—holy and unholy,—all are to be found now among those who call themselves Christians. They sit side by side in our assemblies. They kneel side by side in our pews. They listen side by side to our sermons. They sometimes come up side by side to the Lord's table, and receive the same bread and wine from our hands.

But it shall not always be so. Christ shall come the second time with His fan in His hand. He shall purge His Church, even as He purified the temple. And then the wheat and the chaff shall be separated, and each go to its own place.

Before Christ comes *separation is impossible*. It is not in man's power to effect it. There lives not the minister on earth who can read the hearts of every one in his congregation. About some he may speak decidedly,—he cannot about all. Who have oil in their lamps, and who have not,—who have grace as well as profession, and who have profession only, and no grace,—who are children of God, and who of the devil,—all these are questions which, in many cases, we cannot accurately decide. The fan is not put into our hands.

Grace is sometimes so weak and feeble, that it looks like nature. Nature is sometimes so plausible and well-dressed, that it looks like grace. I believe we should many of us have said that Judas was as good as any of the apostles; and yet he proved a traitor. I believe we should have said that Peter was a reprobate when he denied his Lord; and yet he repented immediately, and rose again. We are but fallible men. We know in part, and prophecy in part. We scarcely understand our own hearts. It is no great wonder if we cannot read the hearts of others.

But it will not always be so. There is One coming who never errs in judgment, and is perfect in knowledge. Jesus shall purge His floor. Jesus shall sift the chaff from the wheat. I wait for this. Till then I will lean to the side of charity in my judgments. I would rather tolerate much chaff in the Church, than cast out one grain of wheat. He shall soon come who has His fan in His hand, and then the certainty about every one shall be known.

Before Christ comes *I do not expect to see a perfect Church*. There cannot be such a thing. The wheat and the chaff, in the present state of things, will always be found together. I pity those who leave one Church and join another, because of a few faults and unsound members. I pity them, because they are fostering ideas which never can be realized. I pity them, because they are seeking that which cannot be found. I see chaff everywhere. I see imperfections and infirmities of some kind in every communion on earth. I believe there are few tables of the Lord, if any, where all the communicants are converted. I often see loud-talking professors exalted as saints. I often see holy and contrite believers set down as having no grace at all. I am satisfied if men are too scrupulous, they may go fluttering about, like Noah's dove, all their days, and never find rest.

Reader, do you desire a perfect Church? You must wait for the day of Christ's appearing. Then, and not till then, you will see a glorious Church, not having spot or wrinkle, or any such thing. Then, and not till then, the floor will be purged.

Before Christ comes *I do not look for the conversion of the world.* How can it be, if He is to find wheat and chaff side by side in the day of His second coming? I believe some Christians expect that missions will fill the earth with the knowledge of Christ, and that little by litte, sin will disappear, and a state of perfect holiness gradually glide in. I cannot see with their eyes. I think they are mistaking God's purposes, and sowing for themselves bitter disappointment. I expect nothing of the kind. I see nothing in the Bible, or in the world around me to make me expect it. I have never heard of a single parish entirely converted to God, in England or Scotland, or of anything like it. And why am I to look for a different result from the preaching of the Gospel in other lands? I only expect to see a few raised up as witnesses to Christ in every nation: some in one place, and some in another. Then I expect the Lord Jesus will come in glory, with His fan in His hand. And when He has purged His floor, and not till then, His kingdom will begin.

No separation and no perfection till Christ comes! This is my creed. I am not moved when the infidel asks me why all the world is not converted, if Christianity is really true? I answer, It was never promised that it would be so in the present order of things. The Bible tells me that believers will always be few, —that corruptions, and divisions, and heresies, will always abound, and that when my Lord returns to earth He will find plenty of chaff.

No perfection till Christ comes! I am not disturbed when men say, "Make all the people good Christians at home before you send missionaries to the heathen abroad." I answer, If I am to wait for that, I may wait for ever. When we have done all at home, the Church will still be a mixed body,—it will contain some wheat and much chaff.

But Christ will come again. Sooner or later there shall be a separation of the visible Church into two companies, and fearful shall that separation be. The

wheat shall make up one company. The chaff shall
make up another. The one company will be all
godly. The other company will be all ungodly.
Each shall be by themselves, and a great gulf
between, that none can pass. Blessed indeed shall
the righteous be in that day! They shall shine like
stars, no longer obscured with clouds. They shall be
beautiful as the lily, no longer choked with thorns.
Wretched indeed will the ungodly be! How corrupt
will corruption be when left without one grain of
salt to season it! How dark will darkness be when
left without one spark of light! Ah, reader, it is
not enough to respect and admire the Lord's people;
you must belong to them, or you will one day be
parted from them for ever. There will be no chaff
in heaven. Many, many are the families where one
will be taken and another left.

Who is there now among the readers of these
pages that loves the Lord Jesus Christ in sincerity?
If I know anything of the heart of a Christian, your
greatest trials are in the company of worldly people,
—your greatest joys in the company of the saints.
Yes: there are many weary days, when your spirit
feels broken and crushed by the earthly tone of all
around you,—days when you could cry with David,
"Woe is me that I dwell in Mesech, and have my
habitation in the tents of Kedar." And yet there
are hours when your soul is so refreshed and revived

by meeting some of God's dear children, that it seems like heaven on earth. Do I not speak to your heart? Are not these things true? See then how you should long for the time when Christ shall come again. See how you should pray daily that the Lord would hasten His kingdom, and say to Him, "Come quickly, Lord Jesus." Then, and not till then, shall be a pure unmixed communion. Then, and not till then, the saints shall all be together, and shall go out from one another's presence no more. Wait a little. Wait a little. Scorn and contempt will soon be over. Laughter and ridicule shall soon have an end. Slander and misrepresentation will soon cease. Your Saviour shall come and plead your cause. And then, as Moses said to Korah, "The Lord will show who are His." *

Who is there among the readers of these pages that knows his heart is not right in the sight of God? See how you should fear and tremble at the thought of Christ's appearing. Alas, indeed, for the man that lives and dies with nothing better than a cloak of religion! In the day when Christ shall purge His floor, you will be shown up and exposed in your true

---

* "This is certain, when the elect are all converted, then Christ will come to judgment. As he that rows a boat, stays till all the passengers are taken into his boat, and then he rows away; so Christ stays till all the elect are gathered in, and then He will hasten away to judgment."—*Thomas Watson,* 1660.

colours. You may deceive ministers, and friends, and
neighbours,—but you cannot deceive Christ. The
paint and varnish of a heartless Christianity will
never stand the fire of that day. The Lord is a God
of knowledge, and by Him actions are weighed. You
will find that the eye which saw Achan and Gehazi,
has read your secrets, and searched out your hidden
things. You will hear those awful words, "Friend,
how camest thou in hither, not having a wedding
garment?" Oh, tremble at the thought of the day
of sifting and separation! Surely hypocrisy is a most
losing game. Surely it never answers to act a part.
Surely it never answers, like Ananias and Sapphira,
to pretend to give God something, and yet to keep
back your heart. It all fails at last. Your joy is
but for a moment. Your hopes are no better than a
dream. Oh, tremble, tremble: tremble, and repent.

Reader, think on these things. Remember my
question. Begin to meditate on it this very day.
Are you wheat or chaff?

III. Let me show you, in the third place, *the
portion which Christ's people shall receive, when He
comes to purge His floor.*

The text at the beginning of this tract tells us
this in good and comfortable words. It tells us that
Christ shall "gather His wheat into His garner."

When the Lord Jesus comes the second time, He

shall collect His believing people into a place of safety. He will send His angels, and gather them from every quarter. The sea shall give up the dead that are in it, and the graves the dead that are in them, and the living shall be changed. Not one poor sinner of mankind who has ever laid hold on Christ by faith shall be wanting in that company. Not one single grain of wheat shall be missing, and left outside, when judgments fall upon a wicked world. There shall be a garner for the wheat of the earth, and into that garner all the wheat shall be brought.

Ah, reader, it is a sweet and comfortable thought, that "the Lord careth for the righteous." But how much the Lord cares for them, I fear is little known, and dimly seen. They have their trials, beyond question,—and these both many and great. The flesh is weak. The world is full of snares. The cross is heavy. The way is narrow. The companions are few. But still they have strong consolations, if their eyes were but open to see them. Like Hagar, they have a well of water near them, even in the wilderness, though they often do not find it out. Like Mary, they have Jesus standing by their side, though often they are not aware of it for very tears.

Bear with me, while I try to tell you something about Christ's care for poor sinners that believe in Him. Alas, indeed, that it should be needful! But we live in a day of weak and feeble statements. The danger of the state of nature is feebly exposed. The privileges of the state of grace are feebly set forth. Hesitating souls are not encouraged. Disciples are not established and confirmed. The man out of Christ is not rightly alarmed. The man in Christ is not rightly built up. The one sleeps on, and seldom has his conscience pricked. The other creeps and crawls all his days, and never thoroughly understands the riches of his inheritance. Truly this is a sore disease, and one that I would gladly help to cure. Truly it is a melancholy thing that the people of God should never go up to mount Pizgah, and never know the length and breadth of their possessions. To be brethren of Christ, and sons of God by adoption, to have full and perfect forgiveness and the renewing of the Holy Ghost, to have a place in the book of life and a name on the breast-plate of the Great High Priest in heaven,— all these are glorious things indeed. But still they are not the whole of a believer's portion. They are upper springs indeed, but still there are nether springs beside.

The Lord *takes pleasure in His believing people.* Though black in their own eyes, they are comely and honourable in His. They are all fair. He sees no spot in them. Their weaknesses and shortcomings do not break off the union between Him and them.

He chose them, knowing all their hearts. He took them for His own with a perfect understanding of all their debts, liabilities, and infirmities, and He will never break His covenant and cast them off. When they fall, He will raise them again. When they wander, He will bring them back. Their *prayers* are pleasant to Him. As a father loves the first stammering efforts of his child to speak, so the Lord loves the poor feeble petitions of His people. He endorses them with His own mighty intercession, and gives them power on high. Their *services* are pleasant to Him. As a father delights in the first daisy that his child picks and brings him, even so the Lord is pleased with the weak attempts of His people to serve Him. Not a cup of cold water shall lose its reward. Not a word spoken in love shall ever be forgotten. He told the Hebrews of Noah's faith,—but not of his drunkenness; of Rahab's faith, —but not of her lie. Oh, reader, it is a blessed thing to be God's wheat!

The Lord *cares for His believing people in their lives.* Their dwelling place is well known. The street, "called strait," where Judas dwelt, and Paul lodged, —the house by the sea-side, where Peter prayed, were all familiar to their Lord. None have such attendants as they have: angels rejoice when they are born again, angels ministers to them, and angels encamp around them. None have such food: their

bread is given them, and their water sure, and they
have meat to eat of which the world knows nothing.
None have such company as they have: the Spirit
dwelleth with them. The Father and the Son come
to them, and make their abode with them. Their
steps are all ordered from grace to glory. They that
persecute them persecute Christ Himself, and they
that hurt them hurt the apple of the Lord's eye.
Their trials and temptations are all measured out by
a wise Physician: not a grain of bitterness is ever
mingled in their cup, that is not good for the health
of their souls. Their temptations, like Job's, are all
under God's control: Satan cannot touch a hair of
their head without their Lord's permission, nor even
tempt them above that which they shall be able to
bear. As a father pitieth his own children, so does
the Lord pity them that fear Him. He never afflicts
them willingly. He leads them by the right way.
He withholds nothing that is really for their good.
Come what will, there is always a needs-be. When
they are placed in the furnace, it is that they may
be purified. When they are chastened, it is that
they may become more holy. When they are pruned,
it is to make them more fruitful. When they are
transplanted from place to place, it is that they may
bloom more brightly. All things are continually
working together for their good. Like the bee they
extract sweetness even out of the bitterest flowers.

Ah, reader, it is a blessed thing to be Christ's wheat !

The Lord *cares for His believing people in their deaths.* Their times are all in the Lord's hand. The hairs of their heads are all numbered, and not one can ever fall to the ground without their Father. They are kept on earth till they are ripe and ready for glory, and not one moment longer. When they have had sun and rain enough, wind and storm enough, cold and heat enough,—when the ear is perfected,—then, and not till then, the sickle is put in. They are all immortal till their work is done. There is not a disease that can loosen the pins of their tabernacle, until the Lord gives the word. A thousand may fall at their right hand, but there is not a plague that can touch them till the Lord sees good. There is not a physician that can keep them alive when the Lord gives the word. When they come to their death-bed, the Everlasting Arms are round about them, and make all their bed in their sickness. When they die, they die like Moses, according to the word of the Lord, at the right time, and in the right way. And when they breathe their last, they fall asleep in Christ, and are at once carried, like Lazarus, into Abraham's bosom. Ah, reader, it is a blessed thing to be Christ's wheat ! When the sun of other men is setting, the sun of the believer is rising. When other men are laying aside their honours, he is putting his on. Death locks the door on the unbeliever, and shuts him out from hope. But death opens the door to the believer, and lets him into paradise.

And the Lord *will care for His believing people in the dreadful day of His appearing*. The flaming fire shall not come nigh them. The voice of the Archangel and the trump of God shall proclaim no terrors to their ears. Sleeping or waking, quick or dead, mouldering in the coffin, or standing at the post of daily duty,—believers shall be secure and unmoved. They shall lift up their heads with joy, when they see redemption drawing nigh. They shall be changed, and put on their beautiful garments in the twinkling of an eye. They shall be caught up to meet the Lord in the air. Jesus will do nothing to a sin-laden world till all His people are safe. There was an ark for Noah when the flood began. There was a Zoar for Lot when the fire fell on Sodom. There was a Pella for early Christians when Jerusalem was besieged. There was a Zurich for English Reformers when Popish Mary came to the throne. And there will be a garner for all the wheat of the earth in the last day. Ah, reader, it is a blessed thing to be Christ's wheat!

I often wonder at the miserable faithlessness of those among us who are believers. Next to the hardness of the unconverted heart, I call it one of the greatest wonders in the world. I wonder that with such mighty reasons for confidence we can still be so full of doubts. I marvel, above all things, how any can deny the doctrine that Christ's people persevere unto the end, and can fancy that He who loved them so as to die for them upon the cross, will ever let them be cast away. I cannot think so. I do not believe the Lord Jesus will ever lose one of His flock. He will not let Satan pluck away from Him so much as one sick lamb. He will not allow one bone of His mystical body to be broken. He will not suffer one jewel to fall from His crown. He and His bride have been once joined in an everlasting covenant, and they shall never never be put asunder. The trophies won by earthly conquerors have often been wrested from them, and carried off; but this shall never be said of the trophies of Him who triumphed for us on the cross. "My sheep," He says, "shall never perish." (John x. 28.) I take my stand on that text. I know not how it can be evaded. If words have any meaning, the perseverance of Christ's people is there.

I do not believe when David had rescued the lamb from the paws of the lion, that he left it weak and wounded to perish in the wilderness. I cannot believe when the Lord Jesus has delivered a soul from the snare of the devil, that He will ever leave that soul to take his chance, and wrestle on in his own feebleness against sin, the devil, and the world.

Reader, I dare be sure, if you were present at a shipwreck, and seeing some helpless child tossing on the waves, were to plunge into the sea, and save him at the risk of your own life,—I dare be sure you would not be content with merely bringing that child safe to shore. You would not lay him down when you had reached the land, and say, "I will do no more. He is weak,—he is insensible,—he is cold: it matters not;—I have done enough. I have delivered him from the waters,—he is not drowned." You would not do it. You would not say so. You would not treat that child in such a manner. You would lift him in your arms. You would carry him to the nearest house. You would try to bring back warmth and animation. You would use every means to restore health and vigour. You would never leave him till his recovery was a certain thing.

And can you suppose the Lord Jesus Christ is less merciful, or less compassionate? Can you think He would suffer on the cross and die, and yet leave it uncertain whether believers in Him would be saved? Can you think He would wrestle with death and hell, and go down to the grave for our sakes, and yet allow our eternal life to hang on such a thread as our poor miserable endeavours.

Oh, no! He does not do so. He is a perfect and complete Saviour. Those whom He loves, He loves unto the end. Those whom He washes in His blood,

He never leaves nor forsakes. He puts His fear into their hearts, so that they shall not depart from Him. Where He begins a work, there He also finishes. All whom He transplants in His garden enclosed on earth, He transplants sooner or later into paradise. All whom He quickens by His spirit, He will also bring with Him when He enters His kingdom. There is a garner for every grain of the wheat. All shall appear in Zion before God.

From false grace men may fall, and that both finally and foully. I never doubt this. I see proof of it continually. From true grace men never do fall totally. They never did, and they never will. If they commit sin, like Peter, they shall repent and rise again. If they err from the right way, like David, they shall be brought back. It is not any strength or power of their own that keeps them from apostasy. They are kept because the power, and love, and promises of the Trinity are all engaged on their side. The election of God the Father shall not be fruitless, the intercession of God the Son shall not be ineffectual, the love of God the Spirit shall not be labour in vain. The Lord shall keep the feet of His saints. They shall all be more than conquerors through Him that loved them. They shall all conquer, and none die eternally.*

* "Blessed for ever and ever be that mother's child whose faith hath made him the child of God. The earth may shake,

Reader, if you have not yet taken up the cross and become Christ's disciple, you little know what privileges you are missing. Peace with God now and glory hereafter,—the Everlasting Arms to keep you by the way, and the garner of safety in the end;—all these are freely offered to you without money and without price. You may say that Christians have tribulations: you forget that they have also consolations. You may say they have peculiar sorrows: you forget they have also peculiar joys. You see but half the Christian life. You see not all. You see the warfare; but not the meat and the wages. You see the tossing and conflict of the outward part of Christianity; you see not the hidden treasures which lie deep within. Like Elisha's servant, you see the enemies of God's children; but you do not, like Elisha, see the chariots and horses of fire which protect them. Oh, judge not by outward appearances! Be sure that the least drop of the water of life is better than all the rivers of the world. Remember the garner and the crown. Be wise in time.

Reader, if you feel that you are a weak disciple, think not that weakness shuts you out from any of

the pillars of the world may tremble under us, the countenance of the heaven may be appalled, the sun may lose his light, the moon her beauty, the stars their glory; but concerning the man that trusteth in God,—what is there in the world that shall change his heart, overthrow his faith, alter his affection toward God, or the affection of God to him?"—*Richard Hooker*. 1585.

the privileges of which I have been speaking. Weak
faith is true faith, and weak grace is true grace;
and both are the gift of Him who never gives in
vain. Fear not, neither be discouraged. Doubt not,
neither despair. Jesus will never break the bruised
reed, nor quench the smoking flax. The babes in
a family are as much loved and thought of as the
elder brothers and sisters. The tender seedlings in
a garden are as diligently looked after as the old
trees. The lambs in the flock are as carefully tended
by the good shepherd as the old sheep. Oh, rest
assured it is just the same in Christ's family, in
Christ's garden, in Christ's flock. All are loved.
All are tenderly thought of. All are cared for. And
all shall be found in His garner at last.

Reader, think on these things. Begin to meditate
on my question this very day. Are you wheat or
chaff?

IV. Let me show you, in the last place, *the portion which remains for all who are not Christ's people.*

The text at the beginning of this tract describes
this in words which should make our ears tingle,—
Christ shall "burn up the chaff with fire unquenchable."

When the Lord Jesus Christ comes to purge His
floor, He shall punish all who are not His disciples
with a fearful punishment. All who are found im-

penitent and unbelieving,—all who have held the truth in unrighteousness,—all who have clung to sin, stuck to the world, and set their affection on things below,—all who are without Christ. All such shall come to an awful end. Christ shall "burn up the chaff."

Their punishment shall be *most severe*. There is no pain like that of burning. Put your finger in the candle for a moment, if you doubt this, and try. Fire is the most destructive and devouring of all elements. Look into the mouth of a blast furnace, and think what it would be to be there. Fire is of all elements most opposed to life. Creatures can live in air, and earth, and water; but nothing can live in fire. Yet fire is the portion to which the Christless and unbelieving will come. Christ will "burn up the chaff with fire."

Their punishment shall be *eternal*. Millions of ages shall pass away, and the fire into which the chaff is cast shall still burn on. That fire shall never burn low and become dim. The fuel of that fire shall never waste away and be consumed. It is "unquenchable fire."

Oh, reader, these are sad and painful things to speak of! I have no pleasure in dwelling on them. I could rather say with the apostle Paul, "I have great sorrow." But they are things written for our learning, and it is good to consider them. They are a part of that Scripture which is all profitable, and they ought to be heard. Painful as the subject of hell is, it is one about which I dare not, cannot, must not be silent. Who would desire to speak of hell-fire if God had not spoken of it? When God has spoken of it so plainly, who can safely hold his peace?

I dare not shut my eyes to the fact, that a deep-rooted infidelity lurks in men's minds on the subject of hell. I see it oozing out in the utter apathy of some: they eat, and drink, and sleep as if there was no wrath to come. I see it creeping forth in the coldness of others about their neighbours' souls: they show little anxiety to pluck brands from the fire. I desire to denounce such infidelity with all my might. Believing that there are terrors of the Lord, as well as the recompense of reward, I call upon all who profess to believe the Bible, to be on their guard.

I know that some do not believe there is any hell at all. They think it impossible there can be such a place. They call it inconsistent with the mercy of God. They say it is too awful an idea to be really true. The devil of course rejoices in the views of such people. They help his kingdom mightily. They are preaching up his old favourite doctrine: "Ye shall not surely die."

I know furthermore that some do not believe that

hell is eternal. They tell us it is incredible that a compassionate God will punish men for ever. He will surely open the prison-doors at last. This also is a mighty help to the devil's cause. "Take your ease," he whispers to sinners: "if you do make a mistake never mind, it is not for ever."

I know also that some believe there is a hell, but never allow that anybody is going there. All people with them are good as soon as they die,—all were sincere,—all meant well,—and all, they hope, got to heaven. Alas, what a common delusion is this! I can well understand the feeling of the little girl who asked her mother where all the wicked people were buried, "for she found no mention on the grave-stones of any except the good."

And I know very well that some believe there is a hell, but never like it to be spoken of. It is a subject that should always be kept back in their opinion. They see no profit in bringing it forward, and are rather shocked when it is mentioned. This also is an immense help to the devil. "Hush, hush!" says Satan, "say nothing about hell." The fowler wishes to hear no noise when he lays his snare. The wolf would like the shepherd to sleep while he prowls round the fold. The devil rejoices when Christians are silent about hell.

Reader, all these notions are the opinions of man. What is it to you and me what man thinks in religion? Man will not judge us at the last day. Man's fancies and traditions are not to be our guide in this life. There is but one point to be settled: "What says the Word of God?"

Do you believe the Bible? Then depend upon it, *hell is real and true.* It is as true as heaven,—as true as justification by faith,—as true as the fact that Christ died upon the cross,—as true as the Dead Sea. There is not a fact or doctrine which you may not lawfully doubt, if you doubt hell. Disbelieve hell, and you unscrew, unsettle, and unpin everything in Scripture. You may as well throw your Bible away at once. From "no hell" to "no God" there is but a series of steps.

Do you believe the Bible? Then depend upon it, *hell will have inhabitants.* The wicked shall certainly be turned into hell, and all the people that forget God. These shall go away into everlasting punishment. The same blessed Saviour who now sits on a throne of grace, will one day sit on a throne of judgment, and men will see there is such a thing as "the wrath of the Lamb." The same lips which now say "Come: come unto Me," will one day say "Depart, ye cursed!" Alas, how awful the thought of being condemned by Christ Himself, judged by the Saviour, sentenced to misery by the Lamb!

Do you believe the Bible? Then depend upon it, *hell will be intense and unutterable woe.* It is vain to

talk of all the expressions about it being only figures
of speech. The pit, the prison, the worm, the fire,
the thirst, the blackness, the darkness, the weeping,
the gnashing of teeth, the second death,—all these
may be figures of speech if you please. But Bible
figures mean something, beyond all question, and
here they mean something which man's mind can
never fully conceive. Oh, reader, the miseries of mind
and conscience are far worse than those of the body!
The whole extent of hell, the present suffering, the
bitter recollection of the past, the hopeless prospect
of the future, will never be thoroughly known except
by those who go there.

Do you believe the Bible? Then depend upon it,
hell is eternal. It must be eternal, or words have no
meaning at all. For ever and ever,—everlasting,—
unquenchable,—never-dying,—all these are expressions used about hell, and expressions that cannot
be explained away. It must be eternal, or the very
foundations of heaven are cast down. If hell has
an end, heaven has an end too. They both stand or
fall together. It must be, or else every doctrine of
the Gospel is undermined. If a man may escape
hell at length without faith in Christ, or sanctification
of the Spirit, sin is no longer an infinite evil, and
there was no such great need for Christ making an
atonement. And where is there warrant for saying
that hell can ever change a heart, or make it fit for

heaven? It must be eternal, or hell would cease to
be hell altogether. Give a man hope, and he will
bear anything. Grant a hope of deliverance, however distant, and hell is but a drop of water. Ah,
reader, these are solemn things! Well said old
Caryl, "FOR EVER is the most solemn saying in
the Bible." Alas, for that day which shall have no
to-morrow! that day when men shall seek death, and
not find it, and shall desire to die, but death shall
flee from them! Who shall dwell with devouring
fire! Who shall dwell with everlasting burnings!

Do you believe the Bible? Then depend upon
it, *hell is a subject that ought not to be kept back.* It
is striking to observe the many texts about it in
Scripture. It is striking to observe that none say so
much about it as our Lord Jesus Christ, that gracious
and merciful Saviour, and the apostle John, whose
heart seems full of love. Truly it may well be doubt-
ed whether we ministers speak of it as much as we
ought. I cannot forget the words of a dying hearer
of Mr. Newton's: "Sir, you often told me of Christ
and salvation; why did you not oftener remind me
of hell and danger?"

Let others hold their peace about hell if they will;
—I dare not do so. I see it plainly in Scripture,
and I must speak of it. I fear that thousands are
on that broad way that leads to it, and I would fain
arouse them to a sense of the peril before them.

What would you say of the man who saw his neighbour's house in danger of being burnt down, and
never raise the cry of "Fire"?   What ought to be
said of us as ministers, if we call ourselves watchmen
for souls, and yet see the fires of hell raging in the
distance, and never give the alarm?   Call it bad
taste, if you like, to speak of hell.   Call it charity
to make things pleasant, and speak smoothly, and
soothe men with constant lullaby of peace.   From
such notions of taste and charity may I ever be
delivered!   My notion of charity is to warn men
plainly of danger.   My notion of taste in the ministerial office, is to declare all the counsel of God.   If
I never spoke of hell, I should think I had kept back
something that was profitable, and should look on
myself as an accomplice of the devil.

Reader, I beseech you, in all tender affection,
beware of false views of the subject on which I have
been dwelling.   Beware of new and strange doctrines
about hell and the eternity of punishment.   Beware
of manufacturing a God of your own, —a God who is
all mercy, but not just,—a God who is all love, but
not holy,—a God who has a heaven for everybody,
but a hell for none,—a God who can allow good and
bad to be side by side in time, but will make no
distinction between good and bad in eternity.   Such
a God is an idol of your own, as really as Jupiter or
Juggernaut,—as true an idol as any snake or croco-

dile in an Egyptian temple,—as true an idol as was
ever moulded out of brass or clay. The hands of
your own fancy and sentimentality have made him.
He is not the God of the Bible, and beside the God
of the Bible there is no God at all. Your heaven
would be no heaven at all. A heaven containing all
sorts of characters indiscriminately, would be miserable discord indeed. Alas, for the eternity of such a
heaven! There would be little difference between it
and hell. Ah, reader, there is a hell! There is a
fire for the chaff! Take heed, lest you find it out to
your cost too late.

Beware of being wise above that which is written.
Beware of forming fanciful theories of your own, and
then trying to make the Bible square in with them.
Beware of making selections from your Bible to suit
your taste,—refusing, like a spoilt child, whatever
you think bitter,—seizing, like a spoilt child, whatever you think sweet. What is all this but taking
Jehoiakim's penknife? What does it amount to but
telling God, that you, a poor short-lived worm, know
what is good for you better than He? It will not do.
It will not do. You must take the Bible as it is.
You must read it all, and believe it all. You must
come to the reading of it in the spirit of a little child.
Dare not to say, "I believe this verse, for I like it.
I reject that, for I do not like it. I receive this,
for I can understand it. I refuse that, for I cannot

reconcile it with my views." Nay! but O man, who
art thou that repliest against God? By what right
do you talk in this way? Surely it were better to
say over every chapter in the Word, "Speak, Lord,
for thy servant heareth." Ah, reader, if men would
do this, they would never deny hell, the chaff, and
the fire.

Think on these things once more. Meditate upon
them. Remember my question, "Are you wheat or
chaff?"

And now, reader, let me say four things in conclusion, and then I have done. I have shown you
the two great classes of mankind, the wheat and the
chaff. I have shown you the separation which will
one day take place. I have shown you the safety of
the Lord's people. I have shown you the fearful
portion of the Christless and unbelieving. I commend these things to your conscience, as in the sight
of God.

1. First of all, settle it down in your mind, that
the things of which I have been speaking are *all real
and true*.

I do believe that many never see the great truths
of religion in this light. I firmly believe that many
never listen to the things they hear from ministers
as realities. They regard it all, like Gallio, as a
matter of names and words, and nothing more,—a

huge shadow,—a formal part-acting,—a vast sham. Macaulay's History of England, Dicken's last Novel, the latest News from France, India, Australia, California, or New York,—all these are things they realize. They feel interested and excited about them. But as to the Bible, and heaven, and the kingdom of Christ, and the judgment day,—these are subjects that they hear unmoved. They do not really believe them. If Layard had dug up at Nineveh anything damaging the truth and authority of the Old Testament Scriptures, it would not have interfered with their peace for an hour.

Reader, if you have unhappily got into this frame of mind, I charge you to cast it off for ever. Whether you mean to hear or forbear, awaken to a thorough conviction that the things I have brought before you are real and true. The wheat, the chaff, the separation, the garner, the fire,—all these are great realities; as real as the sun in heaven,—as real as the paper which your eyes behold. For my part, I believe in heaven, and I believe in hell. I believe in a coming judgment. I believe in a day of sifting. I am not ashamed to say so. I believe them all, and therefore I write as I do. Oh, reader, take a friend's advice, live as if these things were true!

2. Settle it down in your mind, in the second place, that the things of which I write *concern yourself*.

They are your business, your affair, and your concern.

Many, I am satisfied, never look on religion as a matter that concerns themselves. They attend on its outward part, as a decent and proper fashion. They hear sermons. They read religious books. They have their children christened. But all the time they never ask themselves, "What is all this to me?" They sit in our churches like spectators in a theatre, or court of law. They read our writings as if they were reading a report of an interesting trial, or of some event far away. But they do not say to themselves, "I am the man."

Reader, if you have this kind of feeling, depend upon it, it will never do. There must be an end of all this if ever you are to be saved. You are the man I write to, whoever you may be that reads these pages. I write not specially to the rich. I write not specially to the poor. I write to everybody who will read, whatever his rank may be. It is on your soul's account that I am pleading, and not another's. You are spoken of in the text that begins this tract. You are this very day either among the wheat or among the chaff. Your portion will one day either be the garner or the fire. Oh, that men were wise, and would lay these things to heart! Oh, that they would not trifle, dally, linger, live on half-and-half Christians, meaning well, but never acting boldly, and at last awake when it is too late.

3. Settle it down in your mind, in the third place, that if you are willing to be one of the wheat of the earth, *the Lord Jesus Christ is willing to receive you.*

Does any man suppose that Jesus is not willing to see His garner filled? Do you think He does not desire to bring many sons to glory? Oh, but you little know the depth of His mercy and compassion, if you can think such a thought! He wept over unbelieving Jerusalem. He mourns over the impenitent and the thoughtless in the present day. He sends you invitations by my mouth this hour. He invites you to hear and live, to forsake the way of the foolish, and to go in the paths of understanding. "As I live," He says, "I have no pleasure in the death of him that dieth. Turn ye, turn ye, why will ye die?"

Oh, reader, if you never came to Christ for life before, come to Him this very day! Come to Him with the penitent's prayer for mercy and grace. Come to Him without delay. Come to Him while the subject of these pages is still fresh on your mind. Come to Him before another sun rises on the earth, and let the morning find you a new creature.

If you are determined to have the world, and the things of the world,—its pleasures and its rewards,—its follies and its sins,—if you must have your own way, and cannot give up anything for Christ and your soul;—if this be your case, there is but one end before you. I fairly warn you. I plainly tell you. You will sooner or later come to the unquenchable fire.

But if any man is willing to be saved, the Lord Jesus Christ stands ready to save him. "Come unto Me," He says, "weary soul, and I will give you rest. Come, guilty and sinful soul, and I will give you free pardon. Come, lost and ruined sonl, and I will give you eternal life."

Oh, reader, let this message be a word in season. Arise and call upon the Lord! Let the angels of God rejoice over one more saved soul. Let the courts of heaven hear the good tidings that one more lost sheep is found.

4. Settle it down in your mind, last of all, that if you have committed your soul to Christ, *Christ will never allow that soul to perish.*

The Everlasting Arms are round about you. Lean back in them and know your safety. The same hand that was nailed to the cross is holding you. The same wisdom that framed the heavens and the earth is engaged to maintain your cause. The same power that redeemed the tribes from the house of bondage is on your side. The same love that bore with and carried Israel from Egypt to Canaan is pledged to keep you. Ah, reader, they are well kept whom Christ keeps! Our faith may repose calmly on such a bed as Christ's omnipotence.

Take comfort, doubting believer. Why are you cast down? The love of Jesus is no summer-day fountain: no man ever yet saw its bottom. The compassion of Jesus is a fire that never yet burned low; the cold, grey ashes of that fire have never yet been seen. Take comfort. In your heart you may find little cause for rejoicing. But you may always rejoice in the Lord.

You say your faith is so small. But where is it said that none shall be saved except their faith be great? And after all, "Who gave thee any faith at all?" The very fact that you have any faith is a token for good.

You say your sins are so many. But where is the sin, or heap of sins that the blood of Jesus cannot wash away? And after all, "Who told thee thou hadst any sins? That feeling never came from thyself." Blessed indeed is that mother's child who really knows and feels that he is a sinner.

Take comfort, I say once more, if you have really come to Christ. Take comfort, and know your privileges. Cast every care on Jesus. Tell every want to Jesus. Roll every burden on Jesus,—sins,—unbelief,—doubts,—fears,—anxieties,—lay them all on Christ. He loves to see you doing so. He loves to be employed as your High Priest. He loves to be trusted. He loves to see His people ceasing from the vain effort to carry their burdens for themselves.

I commend these things to your notice. Only be among Christ's wheat now, and then as sure as the Bible is true, you shall be in Christ's garner hereafter.

Reader, I heartily pray that this volume may do you good. If it does, I have one request to make. Name the writer before the throne of grace. Pray for me.

Are You an Heir?

ROMANS VIII. 14—17

"*As many as are led by the Spirit of God, they are the sons of God.*

"*For ye have not received the spirit of bondage again to fear; but ye have received the spirit of adoption, whereby we cry, Abba, Father.*

"*The Spirit itself beareth witness with our spirit, that we are the children of God:*

"*And if children, then heirs; heirs of God, and joint heirs with Christ; if so be that we suffer with him, that we may also be glorified together.*"

As soon as you have read the verses of Scripture before your eyes, I invite you to consider a very solemn question,—*Are you an heir of glory?*

Mark well what I am asking. I am not speaking
of matters which only concern the rich, the great,
and the noble. I do not ask whether you are an
heir to money or lands. I only ask whether you are
an heir of glory.

The inheritance I speak of is the only inheritance
really worth having. All others are unsatisfying and
disappointing. They bring with them many cares.
They cannot cure an aching heart. They cannot
lighten a heavy conscience. They cannot keep off
family troubles. They cannot prevent sicknesses,
bereavements, separations, and deaths. But there
is no disappointment among the heirs of glory.

The inheritance I speak of is the only inheritance
which can be kept for ever. All others must be left in
the hour of death, if they have not been taken away
before. The owners of millions of pounds can carry
nothing with them beyond the grave. But it is
not so with the heirs of glory. Their inheritance is
eternal.

The inheritance I speak of is the only inheritance
which is within everybody's reach. Most men can never
obtain riches and greatness, though they labour hard
for them all their lives. But glory, honour, and
eternal life, are offered to every man freely, who is
willing to accept them on God's terms. "Whosoever
will," may be an heir of glory.

Reader, if you wish to have a portion of this

inheritance, you must be a member of that one
family on earth to which it belongs, and that is the
family of all true Christians. You must become one
of God's children on earth, if you desire to have
glory in heaven. I write to persuade you to become
a child of God this day, if you are not one already.
I write to persuade you to make it sure work that
you are one, if at present you have only a vague
hope, and nothing more. None but true Christians
are the children of God. None but the children of
God are heirs of glory. Give me your attention,
while I try to unfold to you these things, and to
show you the lessons which the verses you have
already read contain.

I.   Let me show you *the relation of all true Christians
to God.   They are " sons of God."*

II.   Let me show you *the special evidences of this
relation.*   True Christians are " *led by the Spirit.*"
They have " *the Spirit of adoption.*"   They have the
" *witness of the Spirit.*"   They " *suffer with Christ.*"

III.   Let me show you *the privileges of this relation.*
True Christians are " *heirs of God, and joint heirs with
Christ,*" and shall be " *glorified together* " with *Him.*

I.   First let me show you *the relation of all true
Christians to God.*   They are God's " Sons."

I know no higher and more comfortable word that

could have been chosen. To be servants of God,—to be subjects, soldiers, disciples, friends,—all these are excellent titles. But to be the sons of God, is a step higher still. What says the Scripture? "The servant abideth not in the house for ever, but the son abideth ever." (John viii. 35.)

To be son of the rich and noble in this world,—to be son of the princes and kings of the earth,—this is reckoned a privilege. But to be a son of the King of kings, and Lord of lords,—to be a son of the High and Holy One, who inhabiteth eternity,—this is something higher still. And yet this is the portion of every true Christian.

The son of an earthly parent looks naturally to his father for affection, maintenance, provision, and education. There is a home always open to him. There is a love which no bad conduct can completely extinguish. All these are things belonging even to the sonship of this world. Think then how great is the privilege of that poor sinner of mankind, who can say of God, "He is my Father."

But HOW can sinful men like you and I become sons of God? When do they enter into this glorious relationship? We are not the sons of God by nature. We are not born so when we come into the world. No man has a natural right to look to God as his Father. It is a vile heresy to say that he has. Men are said to be born poets and painters,—but men are

never born sons of God. The Epistle to the Ephesians tells us, "*Ye were by nature children of wrath,
even as others.*" (Ephes. ii. 3.) The Epistle of St.
John says, "*the children of God are manifest, and the
children of the devil: whosoever doeth not righteousness is
not of God.*" (1 John iii. 10.) The Catechism of the
Church of England wisely follows the doctrine of the
Bible, and teaches us to say, "By nature born in
sin, and children of wrath." Yes! we are all rather
children of the devil, than children of God. Sin is
indeed hereditary, and runs in the family of Adam.
Grace is anything but hereditary, and holy men have
not, as a matter of course, holy sons. How then, and
when does this mighty change and translation come
upon men? When and in what manner do sinners
become the sons and daughters of the Lord Almighty?

Men become sons of God in the day that the Spirit
leads them to believe on Jesus Christ for salvation,
and not before.* What says the Epistle to the
Galatians? "*Ye are all the children of God by faith in
Christ Jesus.*" (Gal. iii. 36.) What says the Epistle
to the Corinthians? "*Of him are ye in Christ Jesus.*"
(1 Cor. i. 30.) What says the Gospel of John?
"*As many as received Christ, to them gave He power* (or
privilege) *to become the sons of God, even to them that*

---

* The reader will of course understand that I am not
speaking now of children who die in infancy, or of persons
who live and die idiots.

believe on His name." (John i. 12.) Faith unites the sinner to the Son of God, and makes him one of His members. Faith makes him one of those in whom the Father sees no spot, and is well pleased. Faith marries him to the beloved Son of God, and entitles him to be reckoned among the sons. Faith gives him fellowship with the Father and the Son. Faith grafts him into the Father's family, and opens up to him a room in the Father's house. Faith gives him life instead of death, and makes him instead of being a servant, a son. Show me a man that has this faith in Christ, and whatever be his Church, or denomination, I say that he is a son of God.

Reader, this is one of those points you should never forget. You and I know nothing of a man's sonship *until he believes.* No doubt the sons of God are foreknown and chosen from all eternity, and predestinated to adoption. (Ephes. i. 5.) But, remember, it is not till they are called in due time, and believe,—it is not till then that you and I can be certain they are sons. It is not till they repent and believe, that the angels of God rejoice over them. The angels cannot read the book of God's election. They know not who are His hidden ones in the earth. They rejoice over no man till he believes. But when they see some poor sinner repenting and believing, then there is joy among them,—joy that one more brand is plucked from the burning, and one more son and heir born again to the Father in heaven. But once more I say, you and I know nothing certain about a man's sonship to God *until he believes on Christ*.

Reader, I warn you to beware of the delusive notion, that all men and women are alike children of God, whether they have faith in Christ or not. It is a wild theory which many are clinging to in these days, but one which cannot be proved out of the Word of God. It is a perilous dream, with which many are trying to soothe themselves, but one from which there will be a fearful waking up at the last day.

That God, in a certain sense, is the universal Father of all mankind, I do not pretend to deny. He is the Great First Cause of all things. He is the Creator of all mankind, and in Him alone, all men, whether Christians or heathens, live and move, and have their being. All this is unquestionably true. In this sense Paul told the Athenians, a poet of their own had truly said, " *We are His offspring*." (Acts xvii. 28.) But this sonship gives no man a title to heaven. The sonship which we have by creation, is one which belongs to stones, trees, beasts, or even to the devils, as much as to us.

That God loves all mankind with a love of pity and compassion, I do not deny. His tender mercies are over all His works. He is not willing that any should perish, but that all should come to repentance.

He has no pleasure in the death of him that dieth. All this I admit to the full. In this sense our Lord Jesus tells us, "*God so loved the world, that He gave His only begotten Son, that whosoever believeth in Him should not perish, but have everlasting life.*" (John iii. 16.)

But that God is a reconciled and pardoning Father to any but the members of His Son Jesus Christ, and that any are members of Jesus Christ who do not believe on Him for salvation,—this is a doctrine which I utterly deny. The holiness and justice of God are both against the doctrine. They make it impossible for sinful men to approach God, excepting through a mediator. They tell us that God out of Christ is a consuming fire. The whole system of the New Testament is against the doctrine. That system teaches that no man can claim interest in Christ, unless he will receive Him as his Mediator, and believe on Him as his Saviour. Where there is no faith in Christ, it is presumptuous folly to say that a man may take comfort in God as His Father. *God is a reconciled Father to none but the members of Christ.*

It is nonsense to talk of the view I am now up-holding as narrow-minded and harsh. The Gospel sets an open door before every man. Its promises are wide and full. Its invitations are earnest and tender. Its requirements are simple and clear. Only believe on the Lord Jesus Christ, and whosoever thou art, thou shalt be saved. But to say that proud men, who will not bow their necks to the easy yoke of Christ, and worldly men, who are determined to have their own way and their sins,—to say that such men have a right to claim an interest in Christ, and a right to call themselves sons of God, is absurdity indeed. God offers to be their Father; but He does it on certain distinct terms: they must draw near to Him through Christ. Christ offers to be their Saviour; but in doing it He makes one simple requirement: they must commit their souls to Him, and give Him their hearts. They refuse the terms, and yet dare to call God their Father! They scorn the requirement, and yet dare to hope that Christ will save them! God is to be their Father,—but on their own terms! Christ is to be their Saviour,— but on their conditions! What can be more unreasonable? What can be more proud? What can be more unholy than such a doctrine as this? Beware of it, reader, for it is a common doctrine in these latter days. Beware of it, for it is often speciously put forward, and sounds beautiful and charitable in the mouths of poets, novelists, sentimentalists, and tender-hearted women. Beware of it, unless you mean to throw aside your Bible altogether, and set up yourself to be wiser than God. Stand fast on the old Scriptural ground. *No sonship to God without Christ! No interest in Christ without faith!*

I would to God there was not so much cause for

giving warnings of this kind. I have reason to think they need to be given clearly and unmistakably. There is a school of theology rising up in this day, which appears to me most eminently calculated to promote infidelity, to help the devil, and to ruin souls. It comes to us like Joab to Amasa, with the highest professions of charity, liberality, and love. God is all mercy and love, according to this theology:—His holiness and justice are completely left out of sight! Hell is never spoken of in this theology:—its talk is all of heaven! Damnation is never mentioned:—it is treated as an impossible thing:—all men and women are to be saved! Faith, and the work of the Spirit, are refined away into nothing at all! Everybody who believes anything has faith! Everybody who thinks anything has the Spirit! Everybody is right! Nobody is wrong! Nobody is to blame for any action he may commit! It is the result of his position! It is the effect of circumstances! He is not accountable for his opinions, any more than for the colour of his skin! He must be what he is! The Bible of course is a very imperfect book! It is old-fashioned! It is obsolete! We may believe just as much of it as we please, and no more! Reader, of all this theology, I warn you solemnly to beware. In spite of big swelling words about "liberality," and "charity," and "broad views," and "new lights," and "freedom from bigotry," and so forth, I do believe it to be a theology that leads to hell.

Facts are directly against the teachers of this theology. Let them climb to the tops of mountains, and mark the traces of Noah's flood. Let them go to the shores of the Dead Sea, and look down into its mysterious bitter waters. Let them observe the wandering Jews, scattered over the face of the world. And then let them tell us, if they dare, that God is so entirely a God of mercy and love, that He never does, and never will punish sin.

The conscience of man is directly against these teachers. Let them go to the bedside of some dying child of the world, and try to comfort him with their doctrines. Let them see if their vaunted theories will calm his gnawing, restless anxiety about the future, and enable him to depart in peace. Let them show us, if they can, a few well-authenticated cases of joy and happiness in death without Bible promises, —without conversion,—and without that faith in the blood of Christ, which old-fashioned theology enjoins. Alas, when men are leaving the world, conscience makes sad work of these new systems. Conscience is not easily satisfied in a dying hour that there is no such thing as hell.

Every reasonable conception that we can form of a future state is directly against these teachers. Fancy a heaven which should contain all mankind! Fancy a heaven in which holy and unholy, pure and impure, good and bad, would be all gathered together in one confused mass! What point of union would there be in such a company? What common bond of sympathy and brotherhood? What common delight in a common service? What concord, what harmony, what peace what oneness of spirit could exist? Surely the mind revolts from the idea of a heaven in which there would be no distinction between the righteous and the wicked.—between Pharaoh and Moses, between Abraham and the Sodomites, between Paul and Nero, between Peter and Judas Iscariot, between the man who dies in the act of murder or drunkenness and men like Baxter, Wilberforce, and M'Cheyne! Surely an eternity in such a miserable, confused crowd, would be worse than annihilation itself! Surely such a heaven would be no better than hell!

The interests of all holiness and morality are directly against these teachers. If all men and women alike are God's children, whatever is the difference between them in their lives, and all are alike going to heaven, however different they may be from one another here in the world,—where is the use of labouring after holiness at all? What motive remains for living soberly, righteously, and godly? What does it matter how men conduct themselves, if all go to heaven, and nobody goes to hell? Surely the very heathen of Greece and Rome could teach us something better and wiser than this? Surely a doctrine which is subversive of holiness and morality, and takes away all motives to exertion, carries on the face of it the stamp of its origin. It is of earth, and not of heaven. It is of the devil, and not of God.

The Bible is against these teachers all through. Hundreds and thousands of texts might be quoted which are diametrically opposed to their theories. These texts must be rejected summarily, if the Bible is to square with their views. There may be no reason why they should be rejected,—but to suit the theology I speak of they must be thrown away. At this rate the authority of the whole Bible is soon at an end. And what do they give us in its place? Nothing,—nothing at all! They rob us of the bread of life, and do not give us in its stead so much as a stone.

Reader, once more I warn you to beware of this theology. I charge you to hold fast the doctrine which I have been endeavouring to uphold in these pages. Remember what I have said, and never let it go. No inheritance of glory without sonship to God! No sonship to God without an interest in Christ! No interest in Christ without your own personal faith! This is God's truth. Never forsake it.

Who now among the readers of this volume *desires*

to know whether he is a son of God? Ask yourself this day,—and ask it as in God's sight, whether you have repented and believed. Ask yourself whether you are experimentally acquainted with Christ, and united to Him in heart. If not, you may be very sure you are no son of God. You are not yet born again. You are still in your sins. Your Father in creation God may be, but your reconciled and pardoning Father God is not. Yes, though church and world may agree to tell you to the contrary!—though clergy and laity unite in flattering you,—your sonship is worth little or nothing in the sight of God. Let God be true and every man a liar. Without faith in Christ you are no son of God,—you are not born again.

Who is there among the readers of this volume, who *desires to become a son of God?* Let that person see his sin, and flee to Christ for salvation, and this day he shall be placed among the children. Only acknowledge thine iniquity, and lay hold of the hand that Jesus holds out to thee this day, and sonship, with all its privileges, is thine own. Only confess thy sins, and bring them unto Christ, and God is faithful and just to forgive thee thy sins, and cleanse thee from all unrighteousness. This very day old things shall pass away, and all things become new. This very day thou shalt be forgiven, pardoned, accepted in the beloved. This very day thou shalt have a new name given to thee in heaven. Thou didst take up this book a child of wrath. Thou shalt lie down to-night a child of God. Mark this, if thy professed desire after sonship is sincere,—if thou art truly weary of thy sins, and hast really something more than a lazy wish to be free,—there is real comfort for thee. It is all true. It is all written in Scripture, even as I have put it down. I dare not raise barriers between thee and God. This day I say, Believe on the Lord Jesus Christ, and thou shalt be a son, and be saved.

Who is there among the readers of this volume, that *is a son of God indeed?* Rejoice, I say, and be exceeding glad of your privileges. Rejoice, for you have good cause to be thankful. Remember the words of the beloved Apostle: "*Behold what manner of love the Father hath bestowed upon us, that we should be called the sons of God.*" (1 John iii. 1.) How wonderful, that heaven should look down on earth, —that the holy God should set His affections on sinful man, and admit him into His family! What though the world does not understand you! What though the men of this world laugh at you, and cast out your name as evil! Let them laugh, if they will. God is your Father. You have no need to be ashamed. The Queen can create a nobleman. The bishops can ordain clergymen. But Queen, Lords, and Commons,—bishops, priests, and deacons,—all together cannot, of their own power, make one son of God, or one of greater dignity than a son of God. The man that can call God his Father, and Christ his elder Brother,—that man may be poor and lowly, yet he never need be ashamed.

II. Let me show you, in the second place, the *special evidences of the true Christian's relation to God.*

How shall a man make sure work of his own sonship? How shall he find out whether he is one that has come to Christ by faith and been born again? What are the marks, and signs, and tokens, by which the sons of God may be known? This is a question which all who love eternal life ought to ask. This is a question to which the verses of Scripture I am asking you to consider, like many others, supply an answer.

1. The sons of God, for one thing, are all *led by His Spirit.* What says the Scripture? "As many as are led by the Spirit of God, they are the sons of God." (Rom. viii. 14.)

They are all under the leading and teaching of a power which is Almighty, though unseen,—even the power of the Holy Ghost. They no longer turn every man his own way and walk every man in the light of his own eyes, and follow every man his own natural heart's desire. The Spirit leads them. The Spirit guides them. There is a movement in their hearts, lives, and affections, which they feel, though they may not be able to explain, and a movement which is always more or less in the same direction.

They are led away from sin,—away from self-righteousness,—away from the world. This is the road by which the Spirit leads God's children. Those whom God adopts He teaches and trains. He shows to them their own heart. He makes them weary of their own ways. He makes them long for inward peace.

They are led by Christ. They are led to the Bible. They are led to prayer. They are led to holiness. This is the beaten path along which the Spirit makes them to travel. Those whom God adopts He always sanctifies. He makes sin very bitter to them. He makes holiness very sweet.

It is the Spirit who leads them to Sinai, and first shows them the law, that their hearts may be broken. It is He who leads them to Calvary, and shows them the cross, that their hearts may be bound up and healed. It is He who leads them to Pisgah, and gives them distant views of the promised land, that their hearts may be cheered. When they are taken into the wilderness, and taught to see their own emptiness, it is the leading of the Spirit. When they are carried up to Tabor, and lifted up with glimpses of the glory to come, it is the leading of the Spirit. Each one of God's sons is the subject

of these leadings. Each one yields himself willingly
to them. And each one is led by the right way, to
bring him to a city of habitation.

Reader, settle this down in your heart, and do not
let it go. The sons of God are a people led by the
Spirit of God, and always led more or less in the
same way. Their experience will tally wonderfully
when they compare notes in heaven. This is one
mark of sonship.

2. Furthermore, all the sons of God *have the feelings of adopted children towards their Father in heaven.*
What says the Scripture? "Ye have not received
the Spirit of bondage again to fear; but ye have received the Spirit of adoption, whereby we cry, Abba,
Father." (Rom. viii. 15.)

The sons of God are delivered from that slavish
fear of God, which sin begets in the natural heart.
They are redeemed from that feeling of guilt, which
made Adam hide himself in the trees of the garden,
and Cain go out from the presence of the Lord.
They are no longer afraid of God's holiness, and
justice, and majesty. They no longer feel as if there
was a great gulf and barrier between themselves
and God,—and as if God was angry with them, and
must be angry with them, because of their sins.
From these chains and fetters of soul the sons of
God are delivered.

Their feelings towards God are now those of peace and confidence. They see Him as a Father reconciled in Christ Jesus. They look on Him as a God whose attributes are all satisfied by their great Mediator and Peacemaker, the Lord Jesus,—as a God who is just, and yet the justifier of every one that believeth on Jesus. As a Father, they draw near to Him with boldness. As a Father, they can speak to Him with freedom. They have exchanged the spirit of bondage for that of liberty, and the spirit of fear for that of love. They know that God is holy, but they are not afraid. They know that they are sinners, but they are not afraid. Though holy, they believe that God is completely reconciled. Though sinners, they believe they are clothed all over with Jesus Christ. Such is the feeling of the sons of God.

I allow that some of them have this feeling more vividly than others. Some of them carry about scraps and remnants of the old spirit of bondage to their dying day. Many of them have fits and paroxysms of the old man's complaint of fear returning upon them at intervals. Very few of the sons of God could be found who would not say, if cross-examined, that since they knew Christ they have had very different feelings towards God, from what they ever had before. They feel as if something like the old Roman form of adoption had taken place between themselves and their Father in heaven. They feel as if He had said to each one of them, "Wilt thou be my son?" and as if their hearts had replied, "I will."

Reader, try to grasp this also, and hold it fast. The sons of God are a people who feel towards God in a way that the children of the world do not. They feel no more slavish fear towards Him. They feel towards Him as a reconciled parent. This then is another mark of sonship.

3. But again, the sons of God *have the witness of the Spirit in their conscience*. What says the Scripture? "The Spirit itself beareth witness with our spirit, that we are the children of God." (Rom. viii. 16.)

They have all got something within their hearts, which tells them there is a relationship between themselves and God. They feel something which tells them that old things are passed away, and all things become new,—that guilt is gone,—that peace is restored,—that heaven's door is opened, and hell's door is shut. They have, in short, what the children of the world have not,—a felt, positive, reasonable hope. They have what Paul calls the "seal" and "earnest" of the Spirit. (2 Cor. i. 22; Ephes. i. 13.)

Reader, I do not for a moment deny that this witness of the spirit is exceedingly various in the extent to which the sons of God possess it. With some it is a loud, clear, ringing, distinct testimony of conscience: "I am Christ's and Christ is mine." With others it is a little feeble, stammering whisper, which the devil and the flesh often prevent being heard. Some of the children of God speed on their course towards heaven under the full sails of assurance. Others are tossed to and fro all their voyage, and will scarcely believe they have got faith. But take the least and lowest of the sons of God. Ask him if he will give up the little bit of religious hope which he has attained? Ask him if he will exchange his heart, with all its doubts and conflicts, its fightings, and fears,—ask him if he will exchange that heart for the heart of the downright worldly and careless man? Ask him if he would be content to turn round and throw down the things he has got hold of, and go back to the world? Who can doubt what the answer would be? "I cannot do that," he would reply. "I do not know whether I have faith: I do not feel sure I have got grace: but I have got something within me I would not like to part with." And what is that "*something*"? I will tell you. It is the witness of the Spirit.

Reader, try to understand this also. The sons of God have the witness of the Spirit in their consciences. This is another mark of sonship.

4. One thing more let me add. All the sons of

God *take part in suffering with Christ.* What says the Scripture? "If children, then heirs; heirs of God and joint heirs with Christ; if so be that we suffer with Him." (Rom. viii. 17.)

All the children of God have a cross to carry. They have trials, troubles, and afflictions to go through for the Gospel's sake. They have trials from the world,—trials from the flesh,—and trials from the devil. They have trials of feeling from relations and friends,—hard words, hard conduct, and hard judgment. They have trials in the matter of character,—slander, misrepresentation, mockery, insinuation of false motives,—all these often rain thick upon them. They have trials in the matter of worldly interest. They have often to choose whether they will please man, and lose glory, or gain glory and offend man. They have trials from their own hearts. They have each generally their own thorn in the flesh,—their own home-devil, who is their worst foe. This is the experience of the sons of God.

Some of them suffer more, and some less. Some of them suffer in one way, and some in another. God measures out their portions like a wise physician, and cannot err. But never, I believe, was there one child of God who reached paradise without a cross.

Suffering is the diet of the Lord's family. "Whom the Lord loveth He chasteneth." "If ye be without

chastisement, then are ye bastards, and not sons."
"Through much tribulation we must enter the kingdom of God." (Heb. xii. 6, 8 ; Acts xiv. 22.) When
Bishop Latimer was told by his landlord that he had
never had a trouble, "Then," said he, " God cannot
be here."

Suffering is a part of the process by which the
sons of God are sanctified. They are chastened to
wean them from the world, and make them partakers
of God's holiness. The Captain of their salvation
was made perfect through sufferings, and so are
they. There never yet was a great saint who had
not either great afflictions or great corruptions.
Well said Philip Melancthon, "Where there are no
cares, there will generally be no prayers."

Reader, try to settle this down into your heart
also. The sons of God have all to bear a cross. A
suffering Saviour generally has suffering disciples.
The Bridegroom was a man of sorrows. The bride
must not be a woman of pleasures, and unacquainted
with grief. Blessed are they that mourn. Let us
not murmur at the cross. This also is a sign of
sonship.

Reader, I warn you never to suppose that you are
a son of God except you have the Scriptural marks
of sonship. Beware of a sonship without evidences.
Again I say, Beware. When a man has no leading
of the Spirit to show me,—no Spirit of adoption to

tell of,—no witness of the Spirit in his conscience, —no cross in his experience,—is this a son of God? God forbid that I should say so! His spot is not the spot of God's children. He is no heir of glory.

Tell me not that you have been baptized and taught the Catechism of the Church of England, and therefore *must* be a child of God. I tell you that the parish register is not the book of life. I tell you that to be styled a child of God, and called regenerate in infancy by the faith and charity of the Prayer-book, is one thing;—but to be a child of God indeed, another thing altogether. Go and read that Catechism again. It is a "death unto sin and a new birth unto righteousness," which makes men *children of grace.* Except you know these by experience, you are no son of God.

Tell me not that you are a member of Christ's Church, and so must be a son. I answer that the sons of the Church are not necessarily the sons of God. Such sonship is not the sonship of the eighth of Romans. That is the sonship you must have, if you are to be saved.

And now, I doubt not some reader of these pages will want to know if he may not be saved without the witness of the Spirit.

I answer, if you mean by the witness of the Spirit, the full assurance of hope, you may be so saved without question. But if you want to know whether a man can be saved without any inward sense, or knowledge, or hope of salvation, I answer that ordinarily he cannot. I warn you plainly to cast away all indecision as to your state before God, and to make your calling sure. Clear up your position and relationship. Do not think there is anything praiseworthy in always doubting. Leave that to the Papist. Do not fancy it wise to be ever living like the borderers of old time, on the "debatable ground." "Assurance," said old Dodd, the Puritan, "may be attained, and what have we been doing all our lives since we became Christians if we have not attained it?"

I doubt not some true Christians who read this volume will think their evidence of sonship is too small to be good, and will write bitter things against themselves. Let me try to cheer them. Who gave you the feelings you possess? Who made you hate sin? Who made you love Christ? Who made you long and labour to be holy? Whence did these feelings come? Did they come from nature? There are no such products in a natural man's heart. Did they come from the devil? He would fain stifle such feelings altogether. Cheer up, and take courage. Fear not, neither be cast down. Press forward, and go on. There is hope for you after all. Strive. Labour. Seek. Ask. Knock. Follow on. You shall yet see that you are the sons of God.

III. Let me show you, in the last place, *the privileges of the true Christian's relation to God.*

Nothing can be conceived more glorious than the prospects of the sons of God. The words of Scripture which head this tract, contain a rich mine of good and comfortable things. "If we are children," says Paul, "we are heirs; heirs of God and joint heirs with Christ,—to be glorified together with Him." (Rom. viii. 17.)

True Christians, then, are "heirs,"—something is prepared for them all which is yet to be revealed.

They are "heirs of God." To be heirs of the rich on earth is something. How much more then is it to be son and heir of the King of kings!

They are "joint heirs with Christ." They shall share in His majesty, and take part in His glory. They shall be glorified together with Him.

And this, remember, is for all the children. Abraham took care to provide for all his children,—and God takes care to provide for His. None of them are disinherited. None will be cast out. None will be cut off. Each shall stand in his lot, and have a portion in the day when the Lord brings many sons to glory.

Reader, who can tell the full nature of the inheritance of the saints in light? Who can describe the glory which is yet to be revealed, and given to the children of God? Words fail us. Language falls short. Mind cannot conceive fully, and tongue cannot express perfectly, the things which are comprised in the glory yet to come upon the sons and daughters of the Lord Almighty. Oh, it is indeed a true saying of the Apostle John! "It doth not yet appear what we shall be." (1 John iii. 2.)

The very Bible itself only lifts the veil a little which hangs over this subject. How could it do more? We could not thoroughly understand more if more had been told us. Our constitution is, as yet, too earthly,—our understanding is, as yet, too carnal to appreciate more, if we had it. The Bible generally deals with the subject in negative terms, and not in positive assertions. It describes what there will not be in the glorious inheritance, that thus we may get some faint idea of what there will be. It paints the *absence* of certain things, in order that we may drink in a little the blessedness of things *present*. It tells us that the inheritance is incorruptible, undefiled, and fadeth not away. It tells us that the crown of glory fadeth not away. It tells us that the devil is to be bound, that there shall be no more night, and no more curse, that death shall be cast into the lake of fire, that all tears shall be wiped away, and that the inhabitant shall no more say, "I am sick." And these things are glorious things indeed! No corruption!—No fading! —No withering!—No devil!—No curse of sin!—

No sorrow!—No tears!—No sickness!—No death! Surely the cup of the children of God will indeed run over!

But, reader, there are positive things told us about the glory yet to come upon the heirs of God, which ought not to be kept back. There are many sweet, pleasant, and unspeakable comforts in their future inheritance, which all true Christians would do well to consider. There are cordials for fainting pilgrims in many words and expressions of Scripture, which you and I ought to lay up against time of need.

Is *knowledge* pleasant to us now? Is the little that we know of God, and Christ, and the Bible, precious to our souls, and do we long for more? We shall have it perfectly in glory. What says the Scripture? "Then shall I know, even as also I am known." (1 Cor. xiii. 12.) Blessed be God, there will be no more disagreements among believers! Episcopalians and Presbyterians,—Calvinists and Arminians, —Millennarians and Anti-millennarians,—friends of Establishments and friends of the voluntary system, —advocates of infant baptism and advocates of adult baptism,—all will at length see eye to eye. The former ignorance will have passed away. We shall marvel to find how childish and blind we have been.

Is *holiness* pleasant to us now? Is sin the burden and bitterness of our lives? Do we long for entire conformity to the image of God? We shall have it perfectly in glory. What says the Scripture? Christ gave Himself for the Church, "that He might present it to Himself a glorious Church, not having spot, or wrinkle, or any such thing." (Ephes. v. 27.) Oh, the blessedness of an eternal good-bye to sin! Oh, how little the best of us do at present! Oh, what unutterable corruption sticks, like birdlime, to all our motives, all our thoughts, all our words, all our actions! Oh, how many of us, like Naphtali, are goodly in our words, but, like Reuben, unstable in our works! Thank God, all this shall be changed!

Is *rest* pleasant to us now? Do we often feel faint, though pursuing? Do we long for a world in which we need not be always watching and warring? We shall have it perfectly in glory. What saith the Scripture? "There remaineth a rest for the people of God." (Heb. iv. 9.) The daily, hourly conflict with the world, the flesh, and the devil, shall at length be at an end. The enemy shall be bound. The warfare shall be over. The wicked shall at last cease from troubling. The weary shall at length be at rest. There shall be a great calm.

Is *service* pleasant to us now? Do we find it sweet to work for Christ, and yet groan, being burdened by a feeble body? Is our spirit often willing, but hampered and clogged by the poor weak flesh? Have our hearts burned within us when we have been allowed to give a cup of cold water for Christ's sake, and have we sighed to think what unprofitable servants we are? Let us take comfort. We shall be able to serve perfectly in glory, and without weariness. What saith the Scripture? "They serve Him day and night in His temple." (Rev. vii. 15.)

Is *satisfaction* pleasant to us now? Do we find the world empty? Do we long for the filling up of every void place and gap in our hearts? We shall have it perfectly in glory. We shall no longer have to mourn over cracks in all our earthen vessels, and thorns on all our roses, and bitter dregs in all our sweet cups. We shall no longer lament with Jonah over withered gourds. We shall no longer say with Solomon, "All is vanity and vexation of spirit." We shall no longer cry with aged David, "I have seen an end of all perfection." What saith the Scripture? "I shall be satisfied when I awake with Thy likeness." (Psalm xvii. 15.)

Is *communion with the saints* pleasant to us now? Do we feel that we are never so happy as when we are with the excellent of the earth? Are we never so much at home as in their company? We shall have it perfectly in glory. What saith the Scripture? "The Son of Man shall send His angels, and they shall gather out of His kingdom all things that offend, and them which work iniquity." "He shall send His angels with a great sound of a trumpet, and they shall gather together His elect from the four winds."

(Matt. xiii. 41; xxiv. 31.) Praised be God! we shall see all the saints of whom we have read in the Bible, and in whose steps we have tried to walk. We shall see apostles, prophets, patriarchs, martyrs, reformers, missionaries, and ministers, of whom the world was not worthy. We shall see the faces of those we have known and loved in Christ on earth, and over whose departure we shed bitter tears. We shall see them more bright and glorious than they ever were before. And best of all, we shall see them without hurry and anxiety, and without feeling that we only meet to part again. In glory there is no death, no parting, no farewell!

Is *communion with Christ* pleasant to us now? Do we find His name precious to us? Do we feel our hearts burn within us at the thought of His dying love? We shall have perfect communion with Him in glory. "We shall ever be with the Lord." (1 Thess. iv. 17.) We shall be with Him in paradise. We shall see His face in the kingdom. These eyes of ours will behold those hands and feet which were pierced with nails, and that head which was crowned with thorns. Where He is, there will the sons of God be. When He comes, they will come with Him. When He sits down in His glory, they will sit down by His side. Blessed prospect indeed! I am a dying man in a dying world! All before me is dark! The world to come is a harbour unknown! But Christ is there, and that is enough. Surely if there is rest and peace in following Him by faith on earth, there will be far more rest and peace when we see Him face to face. If we have found it good to follow the pillar of cloud and fire in the wilderness, we shall find it a thousand times better to sit down in our eternal inheritance with our Joshua in the promised land.

Ah, reader, if you are not yet among the sons and heirs, I do pity you with all my heart. How much you are missing! How little true comfort you are enjoying! There you are, struggling on, and toiling in the fire, and wearying yourself for mere earthly ends,—seeking rest, and finding none,—chasing shadows, and never catching them,—wondering why you are not happy, and yet refusing to see the cause, —hungry and thirsty, and empty, and yet blind to the plenty within your reach. Oh, that you were wise! Oh, that you would hear the voice of Jesus, and learn of Him!

Reader, if you are one of those who are sons and heirs, you may well rejoice and be happy. You may well wait, like the boy Patience in Pilgrim's Progress. Your best things are yet to come. You may well bear crosses without murmuring. Your light affliction is but for a moment. The sufferings of this present time are not worthy to be compared with the glory which is to be revealed. When Christ our life appears, then you also shall appear with Him in glory. You may well not envy the transgressor and his prosperity. You are the truly rich. Well said a dying believer in my own parish, "I am more rich than I ever was in my life." You may say, in the spirit of Mephibosheth, when David returned to Jerusalem, "Let the world take all, my King is coming again in peace." You may say as Alexander said when he gave all his riches away, and was asked what he kept for himself, "I have hope." You may well not be cast down by sickness. The eternal part of you is safe and provided for, whatever happens to your body. You may well look calmly on death. It opens a door between you and your inheritance. You may well not sorrow exclusively over the things of the world,—over partings and bereavements.—over losses and crosses. The day of gathering is before you. Your treasure is beyond reach of harm. Heaven is becoming every year more full of those you love, and earth more empty. Glory in your inheritance. It is all your's if you are a son of God. "If we are children, then we are heirs."

And now, reader, in concluding this subject, *let me ask you, Whose child are you?* Are you the child of nature, or the child of grace? Are you the child of the devil, or the child of God? You cannot be both at once. Which are you?

Settle the question, reader, for you must die at last either one or the other. Settle it, reader, for it can be settled, and it is folly to leave it doubtful. Settle it, for the time is short, and the world is getting old, and you are fast drawing near to the judgment seat of Christ. Settle it, for death is nigh, the Lord is at hand; and who can tell what a day may bring forth? Oh, that you would never rest till the question is settled! Oh, that you may never feel satisfied till you can say, "I have been born again. I am a son of God."

Reader, *if you are not a son and heir of God, let me entreat you to become one without delay.* Would you be rich? There are unsearchable riches in Christ. Would you be noble? You shall be a king. Would you be happy? You shall have a peace which passeth understanding, and which the world can never give, and never take away. Oh, come out, and take up the cross, and follow Christ! Come out from among the thoughtless and worldly, and hear the Word of the Lord: "I will receive you, and will be a Father unto you, and ye shall be my sons and daughters, saith the Lord Almighty." (2 Cor. vi. 18.)

Reader, *if you are a son of God, I beseech you to walk worthy of your Father's house.* I charge you solemnly to honour Him in your life: and above all to honour Him by implicit obedience to all His commands, and hearty love to all His children. Labour to travel through the world like a child of God, and heir of glory. Let men be able to trace a family likeness between you and Him that begat you. Live a heavenly life. Seek things that are above. Do not seem to be building your nest below. Behave like a man who seeks a city out of sight, whose citizenship is in heaven, and who would be content with many hardships till he gets home.

Labour *to feel like a son of God* in every condition in which you are placed. Never forget you are on your Father's ground so long as you are here on earth. Never forget that a Father's hand sends all your mercies and crosses. Cast every care on Him. Be happy and cheerful in Him. Why indeed art thou ever sad if thou art the King's son? Why should men ever doubt when they look at you, whether it is a pleasant thing to be one of God's children?

Labour *to behave towards others like a son of God*. Be blameless and harmless in your day and generation. Be a peacemaker among all you know. Seek for your children sonship to God above everything else. Seek for them an inheritance in heaven, whatever else you do for them. No man leaves his children so well provided for, as he who leaves them sons and heirs of God.

Persevere in your Christian calling, if you are a son of God, and press forward more and more. Be careful to lay aside every weight, and the sin which most easily besets you. Keep your eyes steadily fixed on Jesus: Abide in Him. Remember that without Him you can do nothing, and with Him you can do all things. Watch and pray daily. Be steadfast, unmoveable, and always abounding in the work of the Lord. Settle it down in your heart, that not a cup of cold water given in the name of a disciple, shall lose its reward, and that every year you are so much nearer home.

Yet a little time and He that shall come will come, and will not tarry. Then shall be the glorious liberty, and the full manifestation of the sons of God. Then shall the world acknowledge that they were the truly wise. Then shall the sons of God at length come of age. Then shall they no longer be heirs in expectancy, but heirs in possession. And then shall they hear with exceeding joy, those comfortable words, "Come, ye blessed of my Father, inherit the kingdom prepared for you from the foundation of the world." (Matt. xxv. 34.) Surely that day will make amends for all!

That all who read these pages may see the value of the inheritance of glory, and be found at length in possession of it, is my heart's desire and prayer.

"Be Zealous."

GALATIANS IV. 18

"It is good to be zealously affected always in a good thing."

THERE is a subject before your eyes of vast importance. I mean the subject of religious zeal.

It is a subject, like many others in religion, most sadly misunderstood. Many would be ashamed to be thought "zealous." Many are ready to say of zealous people what Festus said of Paul, "They are beside themselves.—they are mad." (Acts xxvi. 24.)

But it is a subject which no reader of the Bible has any right to pass over. If we make the Bible our rule of faith and practice, we cannot turn away from it. We must look it in the face. What says the Apostle Paul to Titus? Christ gave Himself for us, that He might redeem us from all iniquity, and purify unto Himself a peculiar people, *zealous* of good works." (Titus ii. 14.) What says the Lord Jesus to the Laodicean Church? "Be *zealous* and repent." (Rev. iii. 19.)

Reader, I say plainly, I want to plead the cause of zeal in religion. I am not afraid of it. I love it. I admire it. I believe it to be a mighty blessing. I want to strike a blow at the lazy, easy, sleepy Christianity of these latter days, which can see no beauty in zeal, and only uses the word "zealot" as a word of reproach. I want to remind Christians, that "Zealot" was a name given to one of our Lord Jesus Christ's apostles, and to persuade them to be zealous men.

Come now, and give me your attention, while I tell you something about zeal. Listen to me for your own sake,—for the sake of the world,—for the sake of the Church of Christ. Listen to me, and by God's help, I will show you that to be zealous is to be wise.

I. Let me show you, in the first place, *what is zeal in religion*.

II. Let me show you, in the second place, *when a man can be called rightly zealous in religion*.

III. Let me show you, in the third place, *why it is a good thing for a man to be zealous in religion*.

I.   First of all, I propose to bring before you this question, "What is *zeal* in religion?"

Zeal in religion is a burning desire to please God, to do His will, and to advance His glory in the world in every possible way.   It is a desire which no man feels by nature,—which the Spirit puts into the heart of every believer when he is converted,—but which some believers feel so much more strongly than others, that they alone deserve to be called zealous men.

This desire is so strong when it really reigns in a man, that it impels him to make any sacrifice,—to go through any trouble, to deny himself to any amount,—to suffer, to work, to labour, to toil,—to spend himself and be spent, and even to die,—if only he can please God and honour Christ.

A zealous man in religion is pre-eminently *a man of one thing*.   It is not enough to say that he is ear-nest,—hearty.—uncompromising.—thorough-going, —whole-hearted,—fervent in spirit.   He only sees one thing,—he cares for one thing,—he lives for one thing,—he is swallowed up in one thing, and that one thing is to please God.   Whether he lives, or whether he dies,—whether he has health, or whether he has sickness,—whether he is rich, or whether he is poor,—whether he pleases man, or whether he gives offence.—whether he is thought wise, or whe-ther he is thought foolish,—whether he gets blame, or whether he gets praise,—whether he gets honour, or whether he gets shame,—for all this the zealous man cares nothing at all. He burns for one thing, and that one thing is to please God, and to advance God's glory. If he is consumed in the very burning, he cares not for it,—he is content. He feels that like a lamp, he is made to burn, and if consumed in burning, he has but done the work for which God appointed him. Such an one will always find a sphere for his zeal. If he cannot preach, and work, and give money, he will cry, and sigh, and pray. Yes! if he is only a pauper, on a perpetual bed of sickness, he will make the wheels of sin around him drive heavily, by continually interceding against it. If he cannot fight in the valley with Joshua, he will do the work of Moses, Aaron, and Hur, on the hill. If he is cut off from working himself, he will give the Lord no rest till help is raised up from another quarter, and the work is done. This is what I mean, when I speak of zeal in religion.

You know the habit of mind that makes men great in this world,—that makes such men as Alexander the Great, or Julius Cæsar, or Oliver Cromwell, or Peter the Great, or Charles XII., or Marlborough, or Napoleon, or Pitt. You know that they were all men of one thing. They threw themselves into one grand pursuit. They cared for nothing else. They put everything else aside. They counted everything else as second-rate, and of subordinate importance,

compared to the one thing that they put before their
eyes every day they lived. I say that the same habit
of mind applied to the service of the Lord Jesus
Christ, becomes religious zeal.

You know the habit of mind that makes men great
in the sciences of this world,—that makes such men
as Archimedes, or Sir Isaac Newton, or Galileo, or
Ferguson the astronomer, or James Watt. All these
were men of one thing. They brought the powers
of their minds into one single focus. They cared
for nothing else beside. And this was the secret of
their success. I say that this same habit consecrated
to the service of God, becomes religious zeal.

You know the habit of mind that makes men rich,
—that makes men amass mighty fortunes, and leave
millions behind them. What kind of people were
many of the bankers, and merchants, and tradesmen,
who have left a name behind them, as men who ac-
quired immense wealth, and became rich from being
poor? They were all men that threw themselves
entirely into their business, and neglected everything
else for the sake of that business. They gave their first
attention, their first thoughts, the best of their time,
and the best part of their mind, to pushing forward
the transactions in which they were engaged. They
were men of one thing. Their hearts were not divided. They devoted themselves, body, soul, and
mind, to their business. They seemed to live for

nothing else. I say that, if you turn that habit of
mind to the service of God and His Christ, it makes
religious zeal.

Now, reader, this habit of mind,—this zeal was *the
characteristic of all the Apostles.* See for example the
Apostle Paul. Hear him when he speaks to the
Ephesian elders for the last time, "None of these
things move me, neither count I my life dear unto
myself, so that I might finish my course with joy,
and the ministry that I have received of the Lord
Jesus, to testify the Gospel of the grace of God."
(Acts xx. 24.) Hear him again, when he writes to
the Philippians, "This one thing I do; I press toward the mark for the prize of the high calling of
God in Christ Jesus." (Phil. iii. 13.) See him from
the day of his conversion, giving up his brilliant
prospects,—forsaking all for Christ's sake,—and
going forth to preach that very Jesus whom he had
once despised. See him going to and fro throughout
the world from that time,—through persecution,—
through oppression,—through opposition,—through
prisons, —through bonds, —through afflictions, —
through things next to death itself, up to the very
day when he sealed his faith with his blood, and
died at Rome, a martyr for that Gospel which he
had so long proclaimed. This was true religious *zeal.*

This again, was *the characteristic of the early Christians.* They were men "everywhere spoken against."

They were driven to worship God in dens and caves of the earth. They often lost everything in the world for their religion's sake. They generally gained nothing but the cross, persecution, shame, and reproach. But they seldom, very seldom, went back. If they could not dispute, at least they could suffer. If they could not convince their adversaries by argument, at any rate they could die, and prove that they themselves were in earnest. Look at Ignatius cheerfully travelling to the place where he was to be devoured by lions, and saying as he went, "Now do I begin to be a disciple of my master, Christ." Hear old Polycarp before the Roman Governor, saying boldly when called upon to deny Christ, "Four score and six years have I served Christ, neither hath He ever offended me in anything, and how then can I revile my King?" This was true *zeal*.

This again was *the characteristic of Martin Luther*. He boldly defied the most powerful hierarchy that the world has ever seen. He unveiled its corruptions with an unflinching hand. He preached the long-neglected truth of justification by faith, in spite of anathemas and excommunications, fast and thickly poured upon him.

See him going to the Diet at Worms, and pleading his cause before the Emperor, and the Legate, and a host of the children of this world. Hear him saying, when men were dissuading him from going, and reminding him of the fate of John Huss, "Though there were a devil under every tile on the roofs of Worms, in the name of the Lord I shall go forward." This was true *zeal*.

This again was *the characteristic of our own English Reformers*. You have it in our first Reformer, Wicliffe, when he rose up on his sick bed, and said to the friars, who wanted him to retract all he had said against the Pope, "I shall not die, but live to declare the villanies of the friars." You have it in Cranmer, content to die at the stake rather than deny Christ's Gospel, holding forth that hand to be first burned, which in a moment of weakness had signed a recantation, and saying as he held it in the flames, "This unworthy hand!" You have it in old father Latimer, standing boldly on his faggot, at the age of seventy years, and saying to Ridley, "Courage, brother Ridley! we shall light such a candle this day, as, by God's grace, shall never be put out." This was *zeal*.

This again has been *the characteristic of all the greatest Missionaries*. You see it in Mrs. Judson, in Carey, in Morrison, in Schwartz, in Williams, in Brainerd, in Elliott. You see it in none more brightly than in Henry Martyn. This was a man who had reached the highest academical honours that Cambridge could bestow. Whatever profession he chose to follow, he had the most dazzling prospects of success. He turned his back upon it all. He chose to preach the Gospel to poor benighted heathen. He went forth to an early grave, in a foreign land. He said when he got there, and saw the condition of the people, "I could bear to be torn in pieces, if I could but hear the sobs of penitence,—if I could but see the eyes of faith directed to the Redeemer!" This was *zeal*.

But, reader, to look away from all earthly examples,—this, remember, is pre-eminently the characteristic of our Lord and Saviour Jesus Christ Himself. Of Him it was written hundreds of years before He came upon earth, that He was "clad with *zeal* as with a cloak," and "the *zeal* of thine house hath even eaten me." And his own words were, "My meat is to do my Father's will, and to finish His work." (Psalm lxvi. 9 ; Isaiah lix. 17 ; John iv. 34.)

Where shall we begin, if we try to give examples of His zeal ? Where should we end, if we once began ? Trace all the narratives of His life in the four Gospels. Read all the history of what He was from the beginning of His ministry to the end. Surely if there ever was one who was *all zeal*, it was our great Example,—our Head,—our High Priest,—the great Shepherd of our Profession, the Lord Jesus Christ.

Reader, if these things are so, you should not only beware of running down zeal, but you should also beware of allowing zeal to be run down in your presence. It may be badly directed, and then it becomes a curse;—but it may be turned to the highest and best ends, and then it is a mighty blessing. Like fire not well directed, it is a bad master;—but like fire also, if well directed, it is one of the best of servants. Listen not to those people who talk of zeal as weakness and enthusiasm. Listen not to those who see no beauty in missions,—who laugh at all attempts at the conversion of souls,—who call societies for sending the Gospel to the world useless, —and who look upon City Missions, and District Visiting, and Ragged Schools, and Open Air Preaching, as nothing but foolishness and fanaticism. Beware, least in joining a cry of that kind you condemn the Lord Jesus Christ Himself. Beware, lest you speak against Him who has "left us an ensample that we should follow His steps."

Alas, I fear there are many professing Christians who if they had lived in the days when our Lord and His apostles walked upon earth, would have called Him and all His followers enthusiasts and fanatics! There are many, I fear, who have more in common with Annas and Caiaphas,—with Pilate and Herod, —with Festus and Agrippa,—with Felix and Gallio, —than with St. Paul and the Lord Jesus Christ.

II. I pass on now to the second thing I proposed to speak of. *When is a man truly zealous in religion?*

There never was a grace of which Satan has not made a counterfeit. There never was a good coin issued from the mint, but forgers at once have coined something very like it. It was one of Nero's cruel practices first to sew up Christians in the skins of wild beasts, and then bait them with dogs. It is one of Satan's devices to place distorted copies of the believer's graces before the eyes of men, and so to bring the true graces into contempt. No grace has suffered so much in this way as zeal. Of none perhaps are there so many shams and counterfeits abroad. We must therefore clear the ground of all rubbish on this question. We must find out when zeal in religion is really good, and true, and of God.

1. Reader, if zeal be true, it will be a *zeal according to knowledge*. It must not be a blind, ignorant zeal. It must be a calm, reasonable, intelligent principle, which can show the warrant of Scripture for every step it takes. The unconverted Jews had zeal. Paul says, " I bear them record that they have a zeal of God, *but not according to knowledge*." (Rom. x. 21.) Saul had zeal when he was a persecuting Pharisee. He says himself, in one of his addresses to the Jews, " I was *zealous* toward God, as ye all are this day." (Acts xxii. 3.) Manasseh had zeal in the days when he was an idolater. The man who made his own children pass through the fire,—who gave up

the fruit of his body to Moloch, to atone for the sin of his soul,—that man had zeal. James and John had zeal when they would have called down fire on a Samaritan village. But our Lord rebuked them. Peter had zeal when he drew his sword and cut off the ear of Malchus. But he was quite wrong. Bonner and Gardiner had zeal when they burned Latimer and Cranmer. Were they not in earnest? Let us do them justice. They were zealous, though it was for an unscriptural religion. The members of the inquisition in Spain had zeal, when they tortured men, and put them to horrible deaths, because they would not forsake the Gospel. Yes: they marched men and women to the stake in solemn procession, and called it "An act of Faith," and believed they were doing God service. The Hindoos, who used to lie down before the car of Juggernaut, and allow their bodies to be crushed under its wheels;—had not they zeal? The Indian widows, who used to burn themselves on the funeral pile of their deceased husbands,—the Roman Catholics, who persecuted to death the Vaudois and Albigenses, and cast down men and women from rocks and precipices, because they were heretics;—had not they zeal? The Saracens,—the Crusaders,—the Jesuits,—the anabaptists of Munster,—the followers of Joanna Southcote,— had they not all zeal? Yes! Yes! I do not deny it. All these had zeal beyond question. They were all zealous. They were all in earnest. But their zeal was not such zeal as God approves,—it was not a "zeal according to knowledge."

2. Furthermore, if zeal be true, it will be a zeal *from true motives*. Such is the subtlety of the heart, that men will often do right things from wrong motives. Amaziah and Joash, kings of Judah, are striking proofs of this. Just so a man may have zeal about things that are good and right, but from second-rate motives, and not from a desire to please God. And such zeal is worth nothing. It is reprobate silver. It is utterly wanting when placed in the balance of God. Man looks only at the actions. God looks at the motives. Man only thinks of the quantity of work done. God considers the doer's heart.

There is such a thing as zeal from *party spirit*. It is quite possible for a man to be unwearied in promoting the interests of his own Church or denomination, and yet to have no grace in his own heart,—to be ready to die for the peculiar opinions of his own section of Christians, and yet to have no real love to Christ. Such was the zeal of the Pharisees. They "compassed sea and land to make one proselyte, and when he was made, they made him two-fold more the child of hell than themselves." (Matt. xxiii. 15.) This zeal is not true.

There is such a thing as zeal from mere *selfishness*. There are times when it is men's interest to be zealous in religion. Power and patronage are sometimes given to godly men. The good things of the world are sometimes to be attained by wearing a cloak of religion. And whenever this is the case, there is no lack of false zeal. Such was the zeal of Joab, when he served David. Such was the zeal of only too many Englishmen in the days of the Commonwealth, when the Puritans were in power.

There is such a thing as zeal from the *love of praise*. Such was the zeal of Jehu, when he was putting down the worship of Baal. Remember how he met Jonadab the son of Rechab, and said, " Come with me, and see my zeal for the Lord." Such is the zeal that Bunyan refers to in Pilgrim's Progress, when he speaks of some who went " for praise " to mount Zion. Some people feed on the praise of their fellow creatures. They would rather have it from Christians than have none at all.

Ah! reader, it is a sad and humbling proof of man's corruption, that there is no degree of self-denial and self-sacrifice to which men may not go from false motives. It does not follow that a man's religion is true, because he " gives his body to be burned," or because he gives his " goods to feed the poor." The Apostle Paul tells us that a man may do this, and yet not have true charity. It does not

follow because men go into a wilderness, and become
hermits, that therefore they know what true self-
denial is. It does not follow because people immure
themselves in monasteries and nunneries, or become
sisters of charity, and sisters of mercy, that therefore
they know what true crucifixion of the flesh and
self-sacrifice is in the sight of God. All these
things people may do on wrong principles. They
may do them from wrong motives,—to satisfy a secret
pride and love of notoriety,—but not from the true
motive of zeal for the glory of God. All such zeal,
let us understand, is false. It is of earth, and not
of heaven.

3. Furthermore, if zeal be true, it will be a zeal
about things according to God's mind, and sanctioned by
plain examples in God's Word. Take, for one instance,
that highest and best kind of zeal,—I mean zeal for
our own growth in personal holiness. Such zeal will
make a man feel incessantly that sin is the mightiest
of all evils, and conformity to Christ the greatest of
all blessings. It will make him feel that there is
nothing which ought not to be done, in order to keep
up a close walk with God. It will make him willing
to cut off the right hand, or pluck out the right eye,
or make any sacrifice if only he can attain a closer
communion with Jesus. Is not this just what you see
in the Apostle Paul? He says, "I keep under my body

and bring it into subjection : lest that by any means, when I have preached to others, I myself should be a castaway." "I count not myself to have apprehended : but this one thing I do, forgetting those things which are behind, and reaching forth unto those things which are before, I press toward the mark." (1 Cor. ix. 27; Phil. iii. 13, 14.)

Take, for another instance, zeal for the salvation of souls. Such zeal will make a man burn with desire to enlighten the darkness which covers the souls of multitudes, and to bring every man, woman, and child he sees to the knowledge of the Gospel. Is not this what you see in the Lord Jesus ? It is said that He neither gave Himself, nor His disciples, leisure so much as to eat. (Mark vi. 31.) Is not this what you see in the Apostle Paul? He says, "I am made all things to all men, that I might by all means save some." (1 Cor. ix. 22.)

Take, for another instance, zeal against evil practices. Such zeal will make a man hate everything which God hates, and long to sweep it from the face of the earth. It will make him jealous of God's honour and glory, and look on everything which robs Him of it as an offence. Is not this what you see in Phineas, the son of Eleazar?—or in Hezekiah and Josiah, when they put down idolatry ?

Take, for another instance, zeal for maintaining the doctrines of the Gospel. Such zeal will make a man hate unscriptural teaching, just as he hates sin. It will make him regard religious error as a pestilence which must be checked, whatever may be the cost. It will make him scrupulously careful about every jot and tittle of the counsel of God, lest by some omission the whole Gospel should be spoiled. Is not this what you see in Paul at Antioch, when he withstood Peter to the face, and said he was to be blamed? (Gal. ii. 11.) These are the kind of things about which true zeal is employed. Such zeal, let us understand, is honourable before God.

4. Furthermore, if zeal be true, it will be a zeal *tempered with charity and love.* It will not be a bitter zeal. It will not be a fierce enmity against persons. It will not be a zeal ready to take the sword, and to smite with carnal weapons. The weapons of true zeal are not carnal, but spiritual. True zeal will hate sin, and yet love the sinner. True zeal will hate heresy, and yet love the heretic. True zeal will long to break the idol, but deeply pity the idolater. True zeal will abhor every kind of wickedness, but labour to do good, even to the vilest of transgressors. True zeal will warn as St. Paul warned the Galatians, and yet feel tenderly as a nurse, or a mother over erring children. It will expose false teachers, as Jesus did the Scribes and Pharisees, and yet weep tenderly, as Jesus did over Jerusalem, when He came near to it

for the last time. True zeal will be decided as a surgeon dealing with a diseased limb; but true zeal will be gentle as one that is dressing the wounds of a brother. True zeal will speak truth boldly, like Athanasius, against the world, and not care who is offended;—but true zeal will endeavour in all its speaking, to speak the truth in love.

5. Furthermore, if zeal be true, *it will be joined to a deep humility*. A truly zealous man will be the last to discover the greatness of his own attainments. All that he is and does will come so immensely short of his own desires, that he will be filled with a sense of his own unprofitableness, and amazed to think that God should work by him at all. Like Moses, when he came down from the mount, he will not know that his face shines. Like the righteous, in the twenty-fifth chapter of St. Matthew, he will not be aware of his own good works. Dr. Buchanan is one whose praise is in all the Churches. He was one of the first to take up the cause of the perishing heathen. He literally spent himself, body and mind, in labouring to arouse sleeping Christians to see the importance of missions. Yet he says in one of his letters, "I do not know that I ever had what Christians call zeal." Whitefield was one of the most zealous preachers of the Gospel the world has ever seen. Fervent in spirit, instant in season and out

of season, he was a burning and a shining light, and turned thousands to God. Yet he says, after preaching for thirty years, "Lord help me to begin to begin." M'Cheyne was one of the greatest blessings that God ever gave to the Church of Scotland. He was a minister insatiably desirous of the salvation of souls. Few men ever did so much good as he did, though he died at the age of twenty-nine. Yet he says in one of his letters, "None but God knows what an abyss of corruption is in my heart. It is perfectly wonderful that ever God could bless such a ministry." Ah, reader, where there is self-conceit, there is little true zeal!

Reader, I ask you particularly to remember the description of true zeal, which I have just given. Zeal according to knowledge,—zeal from true motives,—zeal warranted by Scriptural examples,—zeal tempered with charity,—zeal accompanied by deep humility,—this is true genuine zeal,—this is the kind of zeal which God approves. Of such zeal, you and I never need fear having too much.

I ask you to remember the description, because of the times in which you live. Beware of supposing that sincerity alone can ever make up true zeal,— that earnestness, however ignorant, makes a man a really zealous Christian in the sight of God. There is a generation in these days which makes an idol of what it is pleased to call "*earnestness*" in religion.

These men will allow no fault to be found with an
"*earnest man.*" Whatever his theological opinions
may be,—if he be but an earnest man, that is enough
for these people, and we are to ask no more. They
tell you we have nothing to do with minute points
of doctrine, and with questions of words and names,
about which Christians are not agreed. Is the man
an earnest man? If he is, we ought to be satisfied. Earnestness in their eyes covers over a multitude of sins. I warn you solemnly to beware of
this specious doctrine. In the name of the Gospel,
and in the name of the Bible, I enter my protest
against the theory, that mere earnestness can make
a man a truly zealous and pious man in the sight of
God.

These idolaters of earnestness would make out that
God has given us no standard of truth and error, or
that the true standard, the Bible, is so obscure, that
no man can find out what truth is by simply going
to it. They pour contempt upon the Word, the
written Word, and therefore they must be wrong.

These idolaters of earnestness would make us condemn every witness for the truth, and every opponent
of false teaching, from the time of the Lord Jesus
down to this day. The Scribes and Pharisees were
in earnest, and yet our Lord opposed them. And
shall we dare even to hint a suspicion that they ought
to have been let alone? Queen Mary, and Bonner,

and Gardiner were in earnest in restoring Popery, and trying to put down Protestantism, and yet Ridley and Latimer opposed them to the death. And shall we dare to say that as both parties were in earnest, both were in the right? Devil-worshippers and idolaters at this day are in earnest, and yet our missionaries labour to expose their errors. And shall we dare to say that earnestness would take them to heaven, and that missionaries to heathen and Roman Catholics had better stay at home? Are we really going to admit that the Bible does not show us what is truth? Are we really going to put a mere vague thing called "earnestness," in the place of Christ, and to maintain that no earnest man can be wrong? God forbid that we should give place to such doctrine! I shrink with horror from such theology. I warn you solemnly to beware of being carried away by it, for it is common and most seductive in this day. Beware of it, for it is only a new form of an old error,—that old error which says that a man "Can't be wrong whose life is in the right." Admire zeal. Seek after zeal. Encourage zeal. But see that your own zeal be true. See that the zeal, which you admire in others, be a zeal "according to knowledge,"—a zeal from right motives,—a zeal that can bring chapter and verse out of the Bible for its foundation. Any zeal but this is but a false fire. It is not lighted by the Holy Ghost.

III. I pass on now to the third thing I proposed to speak of. Let me show you *why it is good for a man to be zealous*.

It is certain that God never gave a man a commandment which it was not man's interest, as well as duty, to obey. He never set a grace before His believing people which His people will not find it their highest happiness to follow after. This is true of all the graces of the Christian character. Perhaps it is pre-eminently true in the case of zeal.

Zeal is *good for a Christian's own soul*. We all know that exercise is good for the health, and that regular employment of our muscles and limbs promotes our bodily comfort, and increases our bodily vigour. Now that which exercise does for our bodies, zeal will do for our souls. It will help mightily to promote inward feelings of joy, peace, comfort, and happiness. None have so much enjoyment of Christ as those who are ever zealous for His glory, —jealous over their own walk,—tender over their own consciences,—full of anxiety about the souls of others,—and ever watching, working, labouring, striving, and toiling to extend the knowledge of Jesus Christ upon earth. Such men live in the full light of the sun, and therefore their hearts are always warm. Such men water others, and therefore they are watered themselves. Their hearts are like a garden daily refreshed by the dew of the

Holy Ghost. They honour God, and so God honours them.

I would not be mistaken in saying this. I would not appear to speak slightingly of any believer. I know that the Lord takes pleasure in all His people. There is not one, from the least to the greatest,—from the smallest child in the kingdom of God, to the oldest warrior in the battle against Satan,—there is not one in whom the Lord Jesus Christ does not take great pleasure. We are all His children;—and however weak and feeble some of us may be, as a father pitieth his children, so does the Lord pity them that love and fear Him. We are all plants of His own planting;—and though many of us are poor, weakly exotics, scarcely keeping life together in a foreign soil,—yet as the gardener loves that which his hands have reared, so does the Lord Jesus love the poor sinners that trust in Him. But while I say this, I do also believe that the Lord takes special pleasure in those who are zealous for Him,—in those who give themselves, body, soul and spirit, to extend His glory in this world. To them He reveals Himself, as He does not to others. To them He shows things that other men never see. He blesses the work of their hands. He cheers them with spiritual consolations, which others only know by the hearing of the ear. They are men after His own heart, for they are men more like Himself than

others.   None have such joy and peace in believing,
—none have such sensible comfort in their religion,
none have so much of heaven upon earth,—none see
and feel so much of the consolations of the Gospel
as those who are zealous, earnest, thorough-going,
devoted Christians.   For the sake of our own souls,
if there were no other reason, it is good to be zealous,
—to be very zealous in our religion.

Reader, as zeal is good for ourselves individually,
so it is also *good for the professing Church of Christ
generally*.   Nothing so much keeps alive true religion
as a leaven of zealous Christians scattered to and fro
throughout a Church.   Like salt, they prevent the
whole body falling into a state of corruption.   None
but men of this kind can revive Churches when ready
to die.   It is impossible to over-estimate the debt
that all Christians owe to zeal.   The greatest mistake
the rulers of a Church can make, is to drive zealous
men out of its pale.   By so doing, they drain out
the life-blood of the system, and hasten on ecclesiastical decline and death.

Zeal is in truth that grace which God seems to
delight to honour.   Look through the list of Christians who have been eminent for usefulness.   Who
are the men that have left the deepest and most in-
delible marks on the Church of their day?   Who
are the men that God has generally honoured to
build up the walls of His Zion, and turn the battle

from the gate? Not so much men of learning and literary talents, as men of zeal.

Bishop Latimer was not such a deeply read scholar as Cranmer or Ridley. He could not quote Fathers from memory as they did. He refused to be drawn into arguments about antiquity. He stuck to his Bible. Yet it is not too much to say that no English reformer made such a lasting impression on the nation as old Latimer did. And what was the reason? His simple zeal.

Baxter, the puritan, was not equal to some of his contemporaries in intellectual gifts. It is no disparagement to say that he does not stand on a level with Manton or Owen. Yet few men probably exercised so wide an influence on the generation in which he lived. And what was the reason? His burning zeal.

Whitefield, and Wesley, and Berridge, and Venn were inferior in mental attainments to Bishops Butler and Watson. But they produced effects on the people of this country which fifty Butlers and Watsons would probably never have produced. They saved the Church of England from ruin. And what was one secret of their power? Their zeal.

These men stood forward at turning points in the history of the Church. They bore unmoved storms of opposition and persecution.—They were not afraid to stand alone. They cared not though their motives were misinterpreted.—They counted all things but loss for the truth's sake.—They were each and all and every one eminently *men of one thing :*—and that one thing was to advance the glory of God, and to maintain His truth in the world. They were all fire, and so they lighted others. —They were wide awake, and so they awakened others.—They were all alive, and so they quickened others.—They were always working, and so they shamed others into working too.—They came down upon men like Moses from the mount.—They shone as if they had been in the presence of God. —They carried to and fro with them, as they walked their course through the world, something of the atmosphere and savour of heaven itself.

There is a sense in which it may be said that zeal is contagious. Nothing is more useful to the professors of Christianity than to see a real live Christian —a thoroughly zealous man of God. They may rail at him.—They may carp at him.—They may pick holes in his conduct. They may look shy upon him. —They may not understand him any more than men understand a new comet, when a new comet appears ; —but insensibly a zealous man does them good. He opens their eyes. He makes them feel their own sleepiness. He makes their own great darkness visible. He obliges them to see their own barrenness. He compels them to think, whether they like it or not—"What are we doing ? Are we no better than mere cumberers of the ground?" It may be sadly true that "one sinner *destroyeth* much good!" but it is also a blessed truth that one zealous Christian can *do* much good. Yes! one single zealous man in a town,—one zealous man in a congregation,—one zealous man in a Society,—one zealous man in a family, may be a great, a most extensive blessing. How many machines of usefulness such a man sets a going! How much Christian activity he often calls into being which would otherwise have slept! How many fountains he opens which would otherwise have been sealed! Verily there is a deep mine of truth in those words of the Apostle Paul to the Corinthians, "Your zeal hath provoked very many." (2 Cor. ix. 2.)

But, as zeal is good for the Church and for individuals, so zeal is *good for the world*. Where would the Missionary work be if it were not for zeal? Where would our City Missions and Ragged Schools be if it were not for zeal? Where would our District-Visiting and Pastoral-Aid Societies be if it were not for zeal? Where would be our Societies for rooting out sin and ignorance, for finding out the dark places of the earth, and recovering poor lost souls? Where would be all these glorious instruments for good if it were not for Christian zeal? Zeal called these institutions into being, and zeal keeps them at work when they have begun. Zeal gathers a few despised

men, and makes them the nucleus of many a powerful Society. Zeal keeps up the collections of a Society when it is formed. Zeal prevents men from
becoming lazy and sleepy when the machine has
grown large, and begins to get favour from the
world. Zeal raises up men to go forth, putting their
lives in their hands, like Moffat and Williams in our
own day. Zeal supplies their place when they are
gathered into the garner, and raises up a constant
succession of labourers to do the Lord's work.

What would become of the ignorant masses who
crowd the lanes and allies of overgrown cities, if it
were not for Christian zeal? Governments can do
nothing with them: they cannot make laws that will
meet the evil. The vast majority of professing Christians have no eyes to see it; like the priest and Levite,
they pass by on the other side. But zeal has eyes to
see, and a heart to feel, and a head to devise, and a
tongue to plead, and hands to work, and feet to
travel, in order to rescue poor souls, and raise them
from their low estate. Zeal does not stand poring
over difficulties, but simply says, "Here are souls
perishing, and something *shall* be done." Zeal does
not shrink back because there are Anakims in the
way: it looks over their heads, like Moses on Pisgah,
and says, "The land *shall* be possessed." Zeal does
not wait for company, and tarry till good works are
fashionable: it goes forward like a forlorn hope, and

trusts that others will follow by and by. Ah, reader,
the world little knows what a debt it owes to Christian zeal! How much crime it has checked! How
much sedition it has prevented! How much public
discontent it has calmed! How much obedience to
law and love of order it has produced! How many
souls it has saved! Yes: and I believe we little
know what might be done if every Christian was a
zealous man How much if ministers were more
like Bickersteth, and Whitefield, and M'Cheyne!
How much if layman were more like Howard, and
Wilberforce, and Thornton, and Nasmith! Oh, for
the world's sake, as well as your own, resolve, labour,
strive to be zealous Christians!

Beware, I beseech you, of checking zeal. Seek it.
Cultivate it. Try to blow up the fire in your own
heart, and the hearts of others, but never, never check
it. Beware of throwing cold water on zealous souls,
whenever you meet with them. Beware of nipping
in the bud this precious grace when first it shoots.
If you are a parent beware of checking it in your
children;—if you are a husband, beware of checking
it in your wife;—if you are a brother, beware of
checking it in your sisters,—and if you are a minister,
beware of checking it in the members of your congregation. It is a shoot of heaven's own planting.
Beware of crushing it, for Christ's sake. Zeal may
make mistakes.—Zeal may need directing.—Zeal

may want guiding, controlling, and advising. Like the elephants on ancient fields of battle, it may sometimes do injury to its own side. But zeal does not need damping in a wretched, cold, corrupt, miserable world like this. Zeal, like John Knox pulling down the Scotch monasteries, may hurt the feelings of narrow-minded and sleepy Christians. It may offend the prejudices of those old-fashioned religionists, who hate everything new, and abhor all change. But zeal in the end will be justified by its results. Zeal, like John Knox, in the long run of life, will do infinitely more good than harm. Oh, reader, there is little danger of there being too much zeal for the glory of God. God forgive those who think there is! You know little of human nature. You forget that sickness is far more contagious than health, and that it is much easier to catch a cold than impart a glow. Depend upon it, the Church seldom needs a bridle, but often needs a spur. It seldom needs to be checked, but often needs to be urged on.

And now, in conclusion, let me try to apply this subject to the conscience of every person who reads this volume. It is a warning subject,—an arousing subject,—an encouraging subject,—according to the state of our several hearts. I wish by God's help to give every reader his portion.

1.   First of all let me offer *a warning* to all who

make no decided profession of religion. There are thousands and tens of thousands, I fear, in this condition. Reader, if you are one, the subject before you is full of solemn warning. Oh, that the Lord in mercy may incline your heart to receive it!

I ask you then in all affection, Where is your zeal in religion? With the Bible before me, I may well be bold in asking. But with your life before me, I may well tremble as to the answer. I ask again, Where is your zeal for the glory of God? Where is your zeal for extending Christ's Gospel through an evil world? Zeal, which was the characteristic of the Lord Jesus,—zeal, which is the characteristic of the angels,—zeal, which shines forth in all the brightest Christians; where is your zeal, unconverted reader,—where is your zeal indeed? You know well it is nowhere at all. You know well you see no beauty in it. You know well it is scorned and cast out as evil by you and your companions. You know well it has no place, no portion, no standing ground, in the religion of your soul. It is not that you know not what it is to be zealous. You have zeal, but it is all misapplied. It is all earthly. It is all about the things of time. It is not zeal for the glory of God. It is not zeal for the salvation of souls. Yes! many a man has zeal for the newspaper, but not for the Bible,—zeal for the daily reading of the "Times," but no zeal for the daily reading of God's blessed

Word. Many a man has zeal for the account book and the business book, but no zeal about the Book of Life, and the last great account; zeal about Australian and Californian gold, but no zeal about the unsearchable riches of Christ. Many a man has zeal about his earthly concerns,—his family, his pleasures, his daily pursuits; but no zeal about God, and heaven, and eternity.

Reader, if this is your case, awake, I do beseech you, to see your gross *folly*. You cannot live for ever. You are not ready to die. You are utterly unfit for the company of saints and angels. Awake! be zealous and repent. —Awake to see the *harm* you are doing. You are putting arguments in the hands of infidels by your shameful coldness. You are pulling down as fast as ministers build. You are helping the devil. Awake! be zealous, and repent. — Awake to see your childish *inconsistency*. What can be more worthy of zeal than eternal things,—than the glory of God,—than the salvation of souls? Surely if it is good to labour for rewards that are temporal, it is a thousand times better to labour for those that are eternal. Awake! be zealous, and repent.—Go and read that long-neglected Bible. Take up that blessed Book which you have, and perhaps never use. Read that New Testament through. Do you find nothing there to make you zealous, to make you earnest about your soul? Go and look at the cross of Christ. Go and see how the Son of God there shed His precious blood for you,—how He suffered and groaned, and died for you,—how He poured out His soul as an offering for sin, in order that you, sinful brother or sister, might not perish, but have eternal life. Go and look at the cross of Christ, and never rest till you feel some zeal for your own soul,—some zeal for the glory of God,—some zeal for extension of the Gospel throughout the world.

2. Let me, in the next place, say something *to arouse* those who make a profession of being decided Christians, and are yet lukewarm in their practice. There are only too many, I regret to say, in this state of soul. Reader, if you are one, there is much in this subject which ought to lead you to searchings of heart.

Let me speak to your conscience. To you also I desire to put the question in all brotherly affection, Where is your zeal?—Where is your zeal for the glory of God, and for extending the Gospel throughout the world? You know well it is very low. You know well that your zeal is a little feeble glimmering spark, that just lives, and no more;—it is like a thing ready to die. Surely there is a fault somewhere, if this is the case. This state of things ought not to be. You, the child of God,—you, redeemed at so glorious a price,—you, ransomed with such precious blood,—you, who are an heir of glory such as no tongue ever yet told, or eye saw; surely you ought to be a man of another kind. Surely your zeal ought not to be so small.

I deeply feel that this is a painful subject to touch upon. I do it with reluctance, and with a constant remembrance of my own unprofitableness. Nevertheless truth ought to be spoken. The plain truth is, that many believers in the present day seem so dreadfully afraid of doing harm that they hardly ever dare to do good. There are many who are fruitful in objections, but barren in actions; rich in wet blankets, but poor in anything like Christian fire. They are like the Dutch Deputies who would never allow Marlborough to venture anything, and by their excessive caution prevented many a victory being won. Truly, in looking round the Church of Christ, a man might sometimes think that God's kingdom had come, and God's will was being done upon earth, so small is the zeal that some believers show. It is vain to deny it. I need not go far for evidence. I point to Societies for doing good to the heathen, the colonies, and the dark places of our own land, languishing and standing still for want of active support. I ask *is this zeal?* I point to thousands of miserable guinea subscriptions which are never missed by the givers, and yet make up the sum of their Christian liberality. I ask *is this zeal?* I point to false doctrine allowed to grow up in parishes and families without an effort being made to check it, while so-called believers look on, and content themselves with wishing it was not so. I ask *is this zeal?* Would the Apostles have been satisfied with such a state of things ? We know they would not.

Reader, if your conscience pleads guilty to any participation in the short-comings I have spoken of, I call upon you, in the name of the Lord, to awake, be zealous, and repent. Let not zeal be confined to Lincoln's Inn, the Temple, and Westminster ;—to banks, and shops, and counting-houses. Let us see the same zeal in the Church of Christ. Let not zeal be abundant to get gold from Australia, and rescue Franklin from thick ribbed ice, but defective to send the Gospel to the heathen, or to pluck Roman Catholics like brands from the fire, or to enlighten the dark places of the colonies of this great land. Never were there such doors of usefulness opened,—never were there so many opportunities for doing good. I loathe that squeamishness which refuses to help religious works if there is a blemish about the instrument by which the work is carried on. At this rate we might never do anything at all. Resist the feeling, reader, if you are tempted by it. It is one of Satan's devices. It is better to work with feeble instruments than not to work at all. At all events, try to do something for God and Christ,—something against ignorance and sin. Give, collect, teach, exhort, visit, pray, according as God enables you. Only make up your mind that all can do something, and resolve that by you, at any rate, something shall be done. If you have only one talent, do not bury it in the ground. Try to live so as to be missed. There is far more to be done in twelve hours than most of us have ever yet done on any day in our lives.

Think of the *precious souls* which are perishing, while you are sleeping. Be taken up with your inward conflicts if you will. Go on anatomizing your own feelings, and poring over your own corruptions, if you are so determined. But remember all this time souls are going to hell, and you might do something to save them by working, by giving, by writing, by begging, and by prayer. Oh, awake, be zealous, and repent.

Think of the *shortness of time*. You will soon be gone. You will have no opportunity for works of mercy in another world. In heaven there will be no ignorant people to instruct, and no unconverted to reclaim. Whatever you do must be done now. Oh, when are you going to begin? Awake! be zealous, and repent.

Think of *the devil*, and his zeal to do harm. It was a solemn saying of old Bernard when he said that "Satan would rise up in judgment against some people at the last day, because he had shown more zeal to ruin souls than they had to save them." Awake! be zealous, and repent.

Think of *your Saviour*, and all His zeal for you.
Think of Him in Gethsemane and on Calvary, shedding His blood for sinners. Think of His life and
death,—His sufferings and His doings. This He has
done for you. What are you doing for Him? Oh,
resolve that for the time to come you will spend and
be spent for Christ. Awake! be zealous, and repent.

3. Last of all let me encourage all readers of
these pages who are truly zealous Christians.

I have but one request to make, and that is *that
you will persevere*. I do beseech you to hold fast
your zeal, and never let it go. I do beseech you
never to go back from your first works, never to leave
your first love, never to let it be said of you that
your first things were better than your last. Beware
of cooling down. You have only to be lazy and sit
still, and you will soon lose all your warmth. You
will soon become another man from what you are
now. Oh, reader! do not think this a needless exhortation.

It may be very true that wise young believers are
very rare. But it is no less true that zealous old
believers are very rare also. Never allow yourself
to think that you can do too much,—that you can
spend and be spent too much for Christ's cause.
For one man that does too much I will show you a
thousand who do not do enough. Rather think that

the night cometh, when no man can work,—and give, collect, teach, visit, work, pray, as if you were doing it for the last time. Lay to heart the words of that noble-minded Jansenist, who said when told that he ought to rest a little, "What should we rest for? have we not all eternity to rest in?"

Fear not the reproach of men. Faint not because you are sometimes abused. Heed it not if you are sometimes called bigot, enthusiast, fanatic, mad man, and fool. There is nothing disgraceful in these titles. They have often been given to the best and wisest of men. If you are only to be zealous when you are praised for it,—if the wheels of your zeal must be oiled by the world's commendation, your zeal will be but short-lived. Care not for the praise or frown of man. There is but one thing worth caring for, and that is the praise of God. There is but one question worth asking about our actions: "How will they look in the day of judgment?"

Reader, I lay these thoughts before you, and I ask you seriously to consider them.

If you are not yet a zealous man, I pray that God may make you one. If you are, I pray that your zeal may increase more and more to your life's end.

George Whitefield

A Lecture delivered before the Church of England Young Mens' Society, in Freemasons' Hall, London, Jan. 26th, 1852.

THERE are some men whose greatness no person of common sense thinks of disputing. They tower above the rest of mankind, like the Pyramids, the Parthenon, and the Colosseum, among buildings. Such men were Luther and Augustine, Gustavus Adolphus and George Washington, Columbus and Sir Isaac Newton. He who questions *their* greatness, must be content to be thought very ignorant, very prejudiced, or very eccentric. Public opinion has come to a conclusion about them—they were great men.

But there are also great men whose reputation

lies buried under a heap of contemporary ill-will and misrepresentation. The world does not appreciate them, because the world does not know their real worth. Their characters have come down to us through poisoned channels. Their portaits have been drawn by the ill-natured hand of enemies. Their faults have been exaggerated. Their excellencies have been maliciously kept back and suppressed. Like the famous sculptures of Nineveh, they need the hand of some literary Layard to clear away the rubbish that has accumulated round their names, and show them to the world in their fair proportions. Such men were Vigilantius and Wickliffe. Such men were Oliver Cromwell and many of the Puritans. And such a man was George Whitefield, about whom I have now to speak.

There are few men whose characters have suffered so much from ignorance and misrepresentation of the truth, as Whitefield's.

That he was a famous Methodist, and ally of John Wesley, in the last century; that he was much run after by ignorant people for his preaching; that many thought him an enthusiast and fanatic,—all this is about as much as most Englishmen know.

But that he was one of the principal champions of Evangelical religion in the eighteenth century in our own country; that he was one of the most powerful and effective preachers that ever lived; that he was a

man of extraordinary singleness of eye and devoted-
ness to the interests of true religion; that he was
a regularly ordained clergyman of the Church of
England, and would always have worked in the
Church, if the Church had not most unwisely shut
him out;—all these are things of which few people
seem aware. And yet, after calm examination of
his life and writings, I am satisfied this is the true
account that ought to be given of George Whitefield.

My chief desire is to enable men in this day to form
a just estimate of Whitefield's worth. I wish to lend
a helping hand towards raising his name from the
undeservedly low place which is commonly assigned
to it. I wish to place him before your eyes as a
noble specimen of what the grace of God can enable
one man to do. I want you to treasure up his name
in your memories, as one of the brightest in that
company of departed saints, who were in that day
patterns of good works, and of whom the world was
not worthy.

I propose, therefore, without further preface, to
give you a hasty sketch of Whitefield's *times*, Whitefield's *life*, Whitefield's *religion*, Whitefield's *preaching*,
and Whitefield's *actual work on earth*.

1. The story of Whitefield's *times*, is one that
should always be told on occasions like the present.
Without it nobody is qualified to form an opinion

either as to the man or his acts. Conduct that in one kind of times may seem rash, extravagant, and indiscreet, in another may be wise, prudent and even absolutely necessary. In forming your opinion of the comparative merits of Christian men, never forget the old rule, "Distinguish between times." Place yourself in each man's position. Do not judge what was a right course of action in other times, by what seems a right course of action in your own.

Now the times when Whitefield lived were unquestionably the worst times that have ever been known in this country, since the Protestant Reformation. There never was a greater mistake than to talk of "the good old times." The times of the eighteenth century, at any rate, were "bad old times" unmistakably. Whitefield was born in 1714. He died in 1770. It is not saying too much to assert, that this was precisely the darkest age that England has passed through in the last three hundred years. Anything more deplorable than the condition of the country as to religion, morality, and high principle, from 1700 to about the era of the French Revolution, it is very difficult to conceive.

The state of things, as regards vital religion in the Established Church, can only be compared to that of a frozen or palsied carcase. *There* were the time-honoured formularies, which the wisdom of the Reformers had provided. *There* were the services

and lessons from Scripture, just in the same order as
we have them now. But as to preaching the Gospel
in the Established Church, there was almost none.
The distinguishing doctrines of Christianity,—the
atonement,—the work and office of Christ and the
Spirit,—were comparatively lost sight of. The vast
majority of sermons were miserable moral essays,
utterly devoid of anything calculated to awaken,
convert, save, or sanctify souls. The curse of black
Bartholomew-day seemed to rest upon our Church.
For at least a century after casting out two thousand
of the best ministers in England, our Establishment
never prospered.

There were some learned and conscientious bishops
at this era, beyond question. Such men were Secker,
and Gibson, and Lowth, and Warburton, and Butler,
and Horne. But even the best of them sadly misunderstood the requirements of the day they lived in.
They spent their strength in writing apologies for
Christianity, and contending against infidels. They
could not see that without the direct preaching of the
essential doctrines of Christ's Gospel, their labours
were all in vain. And as to the majority of the
bishops, they were potent for negative evil, but
impotent for positive good,—giants at stopping what
they thought disorder, but infants at devising anything to promote real order,—mighty to repress over-
zealous attempts at evangelization, but weak to put

in action any remedy for the evils of the age,—
eagle-eyed at detecting any unhappy wight who trod
on the toes of a rubric or canon, but blind as bats to
the flood of indolence and false doctrine with which
their dioceses were everywhere deluged.

That there were many well-read, respectable, and
honourable men among the parochial clergy at this
period, it would be wrong to deny. But few, it is to
be feared, out of the whole number, preached Christ
crucified in simplicity and sincerity. Many, whose
lives were decent and moral, were notoriously Arians,
if not Socinians. Many were totally engrossed in
secular pursuits : they neither did good themselves,
nor liked any one else to do it for them. They hunted;
they shot ; they drank ; they swore; they fiddled ; they
farmed ; they toasted Church and King, and thought
little or nothing about saving souls. And as for the
man who dared to preach the doctrine of the Bible,
the Articles, and the Homilies, he was sure to be set
down as an enthusiast and fanatic.

The state of religion among the Dissenters was
only a few degrees better than the state of the
Church. The toleration which they enjoyed from
William the Third's time, was certainly productive
of a very bad spiritual effect on them as a body. As
soon as they ceased to be persecuted, they appear to
have gone to sleep. The Baptists and Independents
could still point to Gill, and Guyse, and Doddridge,

and Watts, and a few more like-minded men. But the English Presbyterians were fast lapsing into Socinianism. And as to the great majority of Nonconformists, it is vain to deny that they were very different men from Baxter, and Flavel, and Gurnall, and Traill. A generation of preachers arose who were very orthodox, but painfully cold,—very conscientious, but very wanting in spirituality,—very constant in their objections to the Established Church, but very careless about spreading vital Christianity.

I deeply feel the difficulty of conveying to your minds a correct impression of the times when Whitefield lived. I dislike over-statement as much as any one, but I am thoroughly persuaded it is not easy to make an over-statement of this part of my subject.

These were the times when the highest personages in the realm lived openly in ways which were flatly contrary to the laws of God, and no man rebuked them. No courts, I suppose, can be imagined more thoroughly unlike than the courts of George I. and George II., and the court of Queen Victoria.

These where the times when profligacy and irreligion were reputable and respectable things. Judging from the description we have of men and manners in those days, a gentleman might have been defined as a creature who got drunk, gambled, swore, fought duels, and broke the seventh commandment incessantly. And, for all this, no one thought the worse of him.

These were the days when the men whom kings delighted to honour, were Bolingbroke, Chesterfield, Walpole, and Newcastle. To be an infidel or sceptic, —to obtain power by intrigue, and to retain power by the grossest and most notorious bribery,—were considered no disqualifications at this era. Such was the utter want of religion, morality, and high principle in the land, that men such as these were not only tolerated, but praised.

These were the days when Hume the historian put forth his work, became famous, and got a pension. He was notoriously an infidel. These were the days when Sterne and Swift wrote their clever, but most indecent, productions. Both were clergymen, and high in the Church, but the public saw no harm. These were the days when Fielding and Smollet were the popular authors, and the literary taste of high and low was suited by Roderic Random, Peregrine Pickle, Joseph Andrews, and Tom Jones.

These were the days when Knox says, in his History of Christian Philosophy,—"Some of the most learned men,—the most luminous writers on theological subjects,—were *totally ignorant of Christianity*. They were ingenious heathen philosophers, assuming the name of Christians, and forcibly paganizing Christianity for the sake of pleasing the world." These were the days when Archbishop Drummond (1760) could talk of "intricate and senseless questions about the influence of the Spirit, the power of grace, predestination, imputed righteousness, justification without works, and other opinions which have from the beginning perplexed and perverted, debased, defiled, and wounded Christianity." These were the days when Bishop Warburton considered the teaching office of the Holy Ghost to be completed in the Holy Scriptures, and that His sanctifying and comforting offices are chiefly confined to charity. Such were the leading ministers! What must the mass of teachers have been? Such were the *priests* of Whitefield's time! What must have been the *people*?

These were the days when there was an utter dearth of sound theological writing. The doctrines of the Reformers were trampled under foot by men who sat in their chairs. The bread of the Church was eaten by men who flatly contradicted her Articles. The appetites of religious people were satisfied with "Tillotson's Sermons," and the "Whole Duty of Man." A pension of £200 a-year was actually given to Blair, of Edinburgh, for writing his most unchristian sermons. Ask any theological bookseller, and he will tell you that, generally speaking, no divinity is so worthless as that of the eighteenth century.

In fine, these were the days when there was no

Society for promoting the increase of true religion, but the Christian Knowledge Society, and the Society for the Propagation of the Gospel. And even their work was comparatively trifling. Nothing was done for the Jew. Nothing was done for the heathen. Nothing, almost, was done for the colonies. Nothing was done for the destitute parts of our own country. Nothing was done for education. The Church slept. The Dissenters slept. The pulpit slept. The religious press slept. The gates were left wide open. The walls were left ungarded. Infidelity stalked in. The devil sowed tares broad-cast, and walked to and fro. The gentry gloried in their shame, and no man pointed out their wickedness. The people sinned with a high hand, and no man taught them better. Ignorance, profligacy, irreligion and superstition, were to be seen everywhere. Such were the times when Whitefield was raised up.

I know that this is a dreadful picture. I marvel God did not sweep away the Church altogether. But I believe that the picture is not one whit two highly coloured. It is painful to expose such a state of things. But for Whitefield's sake the truth ought to be known. Justice has not been done to him, because the condition of the times he lived in is not considered. The times he lived in were extraordinary times, and required extraordinary means to be used. And whatever quiet men, sitting by their firesides in

1852, may say to the contrary, I am satisfied that Whitefield was just the man for his times.

2. The story of Whitefield's *life*, which forms the next part of this Lecture, is one that is soon told. The facts and incidents of that life are few and simple, and I shall not dwell upon them at any length.

Whitefield was born in 1714. Like many other great men, he was of very humble origin, his father and mother kept the Bell Inn, in the city of Gloucester. Whether there is such an inn now, I do not know. But, judging from Whitefield's account of his circumstances, it must formerly have been a very small concern.

Whitefield's early life seems to have been anything but religious, though he had occasional fits of devout feeling. He speaks of himself as having been addicted to lying, filthy talking, and foolish jesting. He confesses that he was a Sabbath-breaker, a theatre-goer, a card-player, and a romance-reader. All this went on till he was twelve or fifteen years old.

At the age of twelve he was placed at a grammar school in Gloucester. Little is known of his progress there, excepting the curious fact that even then, he was remarkable for his good elocution and memory, and was selected to make speeches before the corporation at their annual visitations.

At the age of fifteen he appears to have become tired of Latin and Greek, and to have given up all hopes of ever becoming more than a tradesman. He ceased to take lessons in anything but writing. He began to assist his mother in the public-house that she kept. At length, he says, "I put on my blue apron, washed mops, cleaned rooms, and, in one word, became a professed common drawer for nigh a year and a half."

But God, who ordereth all things in heaven and earth, and called David from keeping sheep to be a king, had provided some better thing for Whitefield than the office of a pot-boy. Family disagreements interfered with his prospects at the Bell Inn. An old schoolfellow stirred up again within him the desire of going to the University. And at length, after several providential circumstances had smoothed the way, he was launched, at the age of eighteen, at Oxford, in a position at that time much more humbling than it is now, as a Servitor at Pembroke College.

Whitefield's Oxford career seems to have been the turning-point in his life. According to his own journal he had not been without religious convictions for two or three years before he went to Oxford. From the time of his entering Pembroke College, these convictions rapidly ripened into decided Christianity. He became marked for his attendance on all means of grace within his reach. He spent his leisure time in visiting the city prisons, and doing good. He formed an acquaintance with the famous John Wesley, and his brother Charles, which gave a colour to the whole of his subsequent life. At one time he seems to have narrowly escaped becoming a semi-papist, an ascetic, or a mystic. From this he seems to have been delivered, partly by the advice of wiser, and more experienced Christians, and partly by reading such books as Scougal's "Life of God in the Soul of Man," Law's "Serious Call," Baxter's "Call to the Unconverted," and Alleine's "Alarm to Unconverted Sinners." At length, in 1736, at the early age of twenty-two, he was ordained Deacon by Bishop Benson of Gloucester, and began to run that ministerial race in which he never relaxed his exertions till he was laid in the grave.

His first sermon was preached in St. Mary-le-Cript, Gloucester. It was said to have driven fifteen persons mad. Bishop Benson remarked, that he only hoped the madness might continue. He next accepted temporary duty at the Tower Chapel, London. While engaged there, he preached continually in many of the London churches; and among others, in the parish churches of Islington, Bishopgate, St. Dunstan's, St. Margaret, Westminster, and Bow, Cheapside. From the very beginning he attained a degree of popularity such as no preacher, probably before or since, has ever reached. To say that the churches were crowded when he preached, would be saying little. They were literally crammed to suffocation. An eye-witness said, "You might have walked on the people's heads."

From London he removed for a few months to Dummer, a little rural parish in Hampshire, near Basingstoke. From Dummer he sailed for the colony of Georgia, in North America, after visiting Gloucester and Bristol, and preaching to crowded churches in each place. The object of his voyage was to assist the Wesleys in the care of an Orphan House, which they had established in Georgia, for the children of colonists who died there. The management of this Orphan House ultimately devolved entirely on Whitefield, and entailed on him a world of responsibility and anxiety all his life long. Though well meant, it seems to have been a design of very questionable wisdom.

Whitefield returned from Georgia after about two years' absence, partly to obtain Priest's orders, which were conferred on him by Bishop Benson, and partly on business connected with the Orphan House. And now we reach the era in his life when he was obliged, by circumstances, to take up a line of conduct as a minister, which he probably at one time never contemplated, but which was made absolutely necessary by the treatment he received.

It appears, that on arriving in London after his first visit to Georgia, he found the countenances of many of the clergy no longer towards him as they were before. They had taken fright at some expressions in his published letters, and some reports of his conduct in America. They were scandalized at his preaching the doctrine of regeneration in the way that he did, as a thing which many of their parishioners needed. The pulpits of many churches were flatly refused to him. Churchwardens, who had no eyes for heresy and drunkenness, were filled with virtuous indignation about what they called breaches of order. Bishops who could tolerate Arianism, and Socinianism, got into a state of excitement about a man who simply preached the Gospel, and put forth warnings against fanaticism and enthusiasm. In short, Whitefield's field of usefulness within the Church was rapidly narrowed on every side.

The step which seemed to have decided Whitefield's course of action at this period of his life, was his adoption of open-air preaching. He had gone to Islington, on a Sunday in April, 1739, to preach for the vicar, his friend, Mr. Stonehouse. In the midst of the prayers, the churchwarden came to him and demanded his license for preaching in the London diocese. This, Whitefield of course had not got, any more than any clergyman not regularly officiating in the diocese has at this day. The upshot of the matter was, that being forbidden to preach in the pulpit, he went outside, after the service, and preached in the churchyard. From that day, he regularly took up the practice of open-air preaching. Wherever there were large open fields around London, wherever there were large bands of idle, church-despising, Sabbath-breaking people gathered together—there went Whitefield and lifted up his voice. The Gospel so proclaimed, was listened to, and greedily received by hundreds who had never dreamed of visiting a place of worship. In Moor Fields, in Hackney Fields, in Mary-le-bone Fields, in May Fair, in Smithfield, on Kennington Common, on Blackheath, Sunday after Sunday, Whitefield preached to admiring masses. Ten thousand, fifteen thousand, twenty thousand, thirty thousand, were computed sometimes to have heard him at once. The cause of pure religion, beyond doubt, was advanced. Souls were plucked from the hand of Satan, as brands from the burning. But it was going much too fast for the Church of those days. The clergy, with very few exceptions, would have nothing to do with this strange preacher. In short, the ministrations of Whitefield in the pulpits of the Establishment, with an occasional exception, from this time ceased. He loved the Church. He gloried in her Articles and Formularies. He used her Prayer-book with delight. But the Church did not love him, and so lost the use of his services. The plain truth is, the Church of England of that day was not ready for a man like Whitefield. The Church was too much asleep to understand him.

From this date to the day of his death, a period of thirty-one years, Whitefield's life was one uniform employment. From Sunday morning to Saturday night—from the 1st of January to the 31st of December—excepting when laid aside by illness, he was almost incessantly preaching. There was hardly a considerable town in England, Scotland, and Wales, that he did not visit. When churches were open to him, he gladly preached in churches. When chapels only were offered, he cheerfully preached in chapels. When church and chapel alike were closed, he was ready and willing to preach in the open air. For thirty-four years he laboured in this way, always proclaiming the same glorious Gospel, and always, as far as man's eye can judge, with immense effect. In one single Whitsuntide week, after he had been preaching in Moorfields, he received one thousand letters from people under spiritual concern, and admitted to the Lord's table three hundred and fifty persons. In the thirty-four years of his ministry, it is reckoned that he preached publicly eighteen thousand times.

His *journeyings* were prodigious, when the roads and conveyances of his times are considered. Fourteen times did he visit Scotland. Seven times did he cross the Atlantic, backward and forward. Twice he went over to Ireland. As to England and Wales, he traversed every county in them, from the Isle of Wight to Berwick-on-Tweed, and from the Land's End to the North Foreland.

His *regular ministerial work* in London, when he was not journeying, was prodigious. His weekly engagements at the Tabernacle in Tottenham-court Road, which was built for him when the pulpits of the Established Church were closed, were as follows.

Every Sunday Morning he administered the Lord's Supper to several hundred communicants, at half-past six. After this he read prayers, and preached, both morning and afternoon,—preached again in the evening at half-past five,—and concluded by addressing a large society of widows, married people, young men, and spinsters, all sitting separately in the area of the tabernacle, with exhortations suitable to their respective stations. On Monday, Tuesday, Wednesday, and Thursday mornings, he preached regularly at six. On Monday, Tuesday, Wednesday, Thursday and Saturday evenings, he delivered lectures. This, you will observe, made thirteen sermons a-week. And all this time he was carrying on a correspondence with people in almost every part of the world.

That any human frame could so long endure the labour he went through, does indeed seem wonderful. That his life was not shortened by violence, is no less wonderful. Once he was nearly stoned to death by a popish mob in Dublin. Once he was nearly mur-

dered in bed by an angry lieutenant of the navy at
Plymouth. Once he narrowly escaped being stabbed
by the sword of a rakish young gentleman in Moorfields. But he was immortal till his work was done.
He died at last at Newbury Port, in North America,
from a fit of asthma, at the age of fifty-six. His last
sermon was preached only twenty-four hours before
his death. It was an open-air discourse, two hours
long. Like Bishop Jewell, he almost died preaching.
He left no children. He was once married, and the
marriage does not seem to have contributed much to
his happiness. But he left a name far better than
that of sons and daughters. Never, I believe, was
there a man of whom it could be so truly said that
he spent and was spent for God.

3. The story of *Whitefield's religion* is the next part
of the subject that I propose to take up, and unquestionably it is one of no little interest.

What sort of doctrine did this wonderful man
teach? an inquirer may reasonably ask. What were
the standards of faith to which he adhered under the
Bible? What were the peculiar essentials of this
religious teaching of his which was so universally
spoken against in his day?

The answer to all these questions is short and
simple. Whitefield was a real, genuine son of the
Church of England. As such he was brought up in

early youth. As such he was educated at Oxford. As such he preached as long as he was allowed to preach within the Establishment. As such he preached when he was outside. References to the Prayer-book, Articles, and Homilies, abound in all his writings and sermons. His constant reply to his numerous opponents was that HE at any rate was consistent with the formularies of his own Church, and that THEY were not. It is not at all too much to say, that when practically cast out of the Establishment, Whitefield was an infinitely better Churchman than ten thousand of the men who received the tithes of the Church of England, and remained comfortably behind.

Whitefield, no doubt, was not a Churchman of the stamp of Archbishop Laud and his school. He was not the man to put a Romish interpretation on our excellent formularies, and to place Church and Sacraments before Christ. He was not a Churchman of the stamp of Tillotson and the school that followed him. He did not lay aside justification by faith, and the need of grace, for semi-heathen disquisitions about morality and duty, virtue and vice. And he was quite right. Laud and his followers were infinitely beyond the doctrines of our Church. Tillotson and his school fell infinitely below.

But if a Churchman is a man who reads the Articles, and Liturgy, and Homilies, in the sense of the men who compiled them,—if a Churchman is a man who sympathizes with Cranmer, and Latimer, and Hooper, and Jewell,—if a Churchman is a man who honours doctrines and ordinances in the order and proportion in which the Thirty-nine Articles honour them,—if this be the true definition of a Churchman, then Whitefield was the highest style of Churchman,— as true a Churchman as ever breathed. And as for Whitefield's adversaries, they were little better than shams and impostors. They had place and power on their side, but they scarcely deserve to be called Churchmen at all.

Perhaps no better test of Whitefield's religious opinions can be supplied, than the list of authors in divinity which he wrote out for the use of a College connected with his Orphan House in Georgia. Of Churchmen, this list includes the names of Archbishop Leighton, Bishop Hall, and Burkitt; of Puritans—Pool, Owen, and Bunyan; of Dissenters —Matthew Henry and Doddridge; of Scotch Presbyterians—Willison and Boston. All these are men whose praise is even now in all the Churches. These, let us understand, were the kind of men with whom he was of one mind in doctrine.

As to the substance of Whitefield's theological teaching, the simplest account I can give of it is, that it was purely *Evangelical*. There were four main things that he never lost sight of in his sermons.

These four were—man's complete ruin by sin, and consequent natural corruption of heart,—man's complete redemption by Christ, and complete justification before God by faith in Christ,—man's need of regeneration by the Spirit, and ·entire renewal of heart and life,—and man's utter want of any title to be considered a living Christian, unless he is dead to sin, and lives a holy life.

Whitefield had no notion of flattering men, and speaking smooth things to them, merely because they were baptized and called Christians, and sometimes came to church. He only looked at one prominent feature in the thousands he saw around him,—and that was, the general character of their lives. He saw the lives of these multitudes were utterly contrary to the Bible, and utterly at variance with the principles of the Church to which they professed to belong. He waited for nothing more. He looked for no further evidence. He judged of trees by their fruits. He told these thousands at once that they were in danger of being lost for ever.—that they were in the broad way that leads to destruction.—that they were dead, and must be made alive again,—that they were lost, and must be found. He told them that if they loved life, they must immediately repent,—they must become new creatures,—they must be converted,—they must be *born again*. And I believe the Apostles would have done just the same.

But Whitefield was just as full and explicit in setting forth the way to heaven, as he was in setting forth the way to hell. When he saw that men's consciences were pricked and their fears aroused, he would open the treasure-house of gospel mercy, and spread forth before a congregation its unsearchable stores. He would unfold to them the amazing love of God the Father to a fallen world—that love from which He gave His only-begotten Son, and on account of which, while we were yet sinners Christ died for us. He would show them the amazing love of God the Son in taking our nature on Him, and suffering for us, the just for the unjust. He would tell them of Jesus, able to save to the uttermost all that would come to God by Him—Jesus and His everlasting righteousness, in which the vilest sinners might stand complete and perfect before the throne of God—Jesus and the blood of sprinkling, which could wash the blackest sins away—Jesus, the High Priest, waiting to receive all who would come to Him, and not only mighty, but ready to save. And all this glorious salvation, he would tell them was close to them. It was not far above them like heaven. It was not deep beneath them like hell. It was near at hand. It was within their reach. He would urge them at once to accept it. The man that felt his sins and desired deliverance, had only to believe and be saved; to ask, and receive; to wash, and be clean. And was he not right to say so? I believe the Apostles would have said much the same.

But while Whitefield addressed the careless and ungodly masses in this style, he never failed to urge on those who made a high profession of religion their responsibility, and to stir them up to walk worthy of their high calling. He never tolerated men who talked well about religion, but lived inconsistent lives. Such men, no doubt there were about him, but it is pretty certain they got no quarter from him. On the contrary, one of his biographers tells us that he was especially careful to impress on all the members of his congregation, the absolute necessity of adorning the doctrine of God in all the relations of life. Masters and servants, rich people and poor, old and young, married and single, each and all were plainly exhorted to glorify God in their respective positions. One day he would tell the young men of his congregation to beware of being like one he heard of, whose uncle described him as such a jumble of religion and business, that he was fit for neither. Another day he would hold up the example of a widow, remarkable for her confidence in God. Another day he would say to them, "God convert you more and more every hour of the day; God convert you from lying a-bed in the morning; God convert you from lukewarmness; God convert you from conformity to the world." Another day he would warn young men against leaving their religion behind them as they rose in the world. "Beware," he would say, "of being golden apprentices, silver journeymen, and copper masters." In short, there was never a greater mistake than to suppose there was anything Antinomian or licentious in Whitefield's teaching. It was discriminating unquestionably. Sinners had their portion : but saints had their portion too. And what was this but walking in the very steps of the Apostle Paul?

The crowning excellence of Whitefield's teaching was, that he just spoke of men, things, and doctrines, in the way that the Bible speaks of them. God, Christ, and the Spirit,—sin, justification, conversion, and sanctification,—impenitent sinners the most miserable of people,—believing saints the most privileged of people,—the world a vain and empty thing, —heaven the only rest for an immortal soul,—the devil a tremendous and ever-watchful foe,—holiness the only true happiness,—hell a real and certain portion for the unconverted ;—these were the kind of things which filled Whitefield's mind, and formed the staple of his ministry. To say that he undervalued the sacraments would be simply false. His weekly communions at the tabernacle are an answer that speaks for itself. But he never put the first things in Christianity second, and the second first. He never put doctrine below sacraments, and sacraments above doctrine. And who shall dare to blame him for this? He only followed the proportion of the Bible.

It is only fair to add, that Whitefield exemplified in his practice the religion that he preached. He had faults, unquestionably: I have not come here to make him out a perfect being. He often erred in judgment: he was often hasty, both with his tongue and with his pen. He had no business to say that Archbishop Tillotson knew no more of religion than Mahomet: he was wrong to set down some people as the Lord's enemies, and others as the Lord's friends, so precipitately as he sometimes did. He was to blame for styling many of the clergy "letter-learned Pharisees," because they could not receive the doctrine of the new birth. But still, after all this has been said, there can be no doubt that in the main, he was a holy, self-denying, and consistent man. Even his worst enemies can say nothing to the contrary.

He was, to the very end, a man of *eminent self-denial*. His style of living was most simple. He refused money when it was pressed upon him, and once to the amount of £7000. He amassed no fortune: he founded no wealthy family. The little money he left behind him at his death arose entirely from the legacies of friends.

He was a man of remarkable *disinterestedness* and singleness of eye. He seemed to live only for two objects,—the glory of God, and the salvation of immortal souls. He raised no party of followers who took his name. He established no system, like Wesley, of which his own writings should be cardinal elements. A frequent expression of his is most characteristic of the man: "Let the name of George Whitefield perish, so long as Christ only is exalted."

Last, but not least, he was a man of *extraordinary catholicity* and liberality in his religion. He knew nothing of that narrow-minded policy which prompts a man to fancy that everything must be barren outside his own camp, and that his party has got a monopoly of truth and heaven. He loved all who loved the Lord Jesus Christ in sincerity. He measured all by the measure which the angels of God use,—"Did they possess repentance towards God, faith towards the Lord Jesus Christ, holiness of conversation?" If they did, they were as his brethren. His soul was with such men, by whatever name they were called. Minor differences were wood, hay, and stubble to him. The marks of the Lord Jesus were the only marks he cared for. This catholicity is the more remarkable, when the spirit of the times he lived in is considered. Even the Erskines, in Scotland, wanted him to preach for no other denomination but their own, viz., the Secession Church. He asked them, "Why only for them?"—and received the notable answer, that "they were the Lord's peo-

ple." This was more than Whitefield could stand.
He asked if there were no other Lord's people but
themselves? He told them, "If all others were the
devil's people, they certainly had more need to be
preached to." And he wound up by informing them,
that "if the Pope himself would lend him his pulpit,
he would gladly proclaim the righteousness of Christ
in it." To this catholicity of spirit he adhered all
his days. And nothing could be a more weighty
testimony against all narrowness of spirit among
believers, than his request shortly before his death,
that when he did die, John Wesley might be asked
to preach his funeral sermon. Wesley and he had
long ceased to see eye to eye on Calvinistic points.
But as Calvin *said* of Luther, so Whitefield was resolved to *think* of Wesley. He was determined to
sink minor differences, and to "know him only as a
good servant of Jesus Christ."

Such was George Whitefield's religion. Comment,
I hope, is needless upon it. Time, at any rate, for-
bids me to dwell on it a moment longer. But surely
I think I have shown enough to justify me in ex-
pressing a wish that we had many living ministers
in the Church of England like George Whitefield.

4. The next part of this evening's subject is one
which I feel some difficulty in handling,—I allude
to Whitefield's *preaching*.

I find that this point is one on which much difference of opinion prevails. I find many are disposed to think that part of Whitefield's success is attributable to the novelty of the Gospel doctrines at the time when he preached, and part to the extraordinary gifts of voice and delivery with which he was endowed, and that the matter and style of his sermons were in nowise remarkable. From this opinion I am inclined to dissent altogether. After calm examination, I have come to the conclusion that Whitefield was one of the most powerful and extraordinary preachers the world has ever seen. My belief is, that hitherto he has never been too highly estimated, and that, on the contrary, he does not receive the credit he deserves.

One thing is abundantly clear and beyond dispute, and that is, that his sermons were wonderfully effective. No preacher has ever succeeded in arresting the attention of such enormous crowds of people, as those he addressed continually in the neighbourhood of London. No preacher has ever been so universally popular in every country he visited.—England, Scotland, and America,—as he was. No preacher has ever retained his hold on his hearers so entirely as he did for thirty-four years. His popularity never waned. It was as great at the end of his days, as it was at the beginning. This of itself is a great fact. To command the ear of people for thirty-four

long years, and be preaching incessantly the whole
time, is something that the novelty of the Gospel
alone will not account for. The theory that his
preaching was popular, because new, to my mind is
utterly unsatisfactory.

Another thing is no less indisputable about his
preaching, and that is, that it produced a powerful
effect on people in every rank of life. He won the
suffrages of high as well as low, of rich as well
as poor, of learned as well as unlearned. If his
preaching had been popular with none but the uneducated masses, we might have thought it possible
there was little in it except a striking delivery and
a loud voice. But facts are, unfortunately, against
this theory too; and under the pressure of these
facts, it will be found to break down.

It is a fact, that numbers of the nobility and gentry of Whitefield's day were warm admirers of his
preaching. The Marquis of Lothian, the Earl of Le-
van, the Earl of Buchan, Lord Rae, Lord Dartmouth,
Lord James A. Gordon, might be named, among
others, besides Lady Huntingdon and a host of ladies.

It is a fact, that eminent statesmen, like Bolingbroke and Chesterfield, were frequently his delighted
hearers. Even the artificial Chesterfield was known
to warm under Whitefield's eloquence. Bolingbroke
has placed on record his opinion, and said, " He is
the most extraordinary man in our times. He has

the most commanding eloquence I ever heard in any person."

It is a fact, that cool-headed men, like Hume the historian, and Franklin the philosopher, spoke in no measured terms of his preaching powers. Franklin has written a long account of the effect his sermons produced at Philadelphia. Hume declared that it was worth going twenty miles to hear him.

Now these are facts—simple, historical, and well-authenticated facts. What shall we say to them? I say that these facts are quite enough to prove that Whitefield's effectiveness was not owing entirely to delivery and voice, as some men would have us believe. Bolingbroke and Chesterfield, and Hume and Franklin, were not such weak men as to allow their judgments to be biassed by any mere external endowments. They were no mean judges of eloquence. They were, probably, among the best qualified critics of the day. And I say confidently, that their opinion can only be explained by the fact, that Whitefield was indeed a most powerful and extraordinary preacher.

But still, after all, the question remains to be answered, What was the secret of Whitefield's unparalleled success as a preacher? How are we to account for his sermons producing effects which no sermons, before or after his time, have ever yet done? These are questions you have a right to ask. But

they are questions I find it very hard to answer.
That his sermons were not mere voice and rant, I
think we have pretty clearly proved. That he was
a man of commanding intellect and grasp of mind,
no one has ever pretended to say. How then are we
to account for the effectiveness of his preaching?

The reader who turns for a solution of this question to the seventy-five sermons published under his
name, will probably be much disappointed. He will
not find in them many striking thoughts. He will
not discover in them any new exhibitions of Gospel
doctrine. The plain truth is, that by far the greater
part of them were taken down in short-hand by
reporters, without Whitefield's knowledge, and published without correction. No intelligent reader, I
think, can help discovering that these reporters
were, most unhappily, ignorant alike of stopping
and paragraphing, of grammar and of Gospel. The
consequence is, that many passages in these sermons
are what Latimer would call a "mingle-mangle," or
what we should call, in familiar language in this
day, "a complete mess."

Nevertheless, I am bold to say, that with all their
faults, Whitefield's printed sermons will repay a
candid perusal. Let the reader only remember what
I have just said, that most of them are miserably
reported, paragraphed, and stopped, and let him
make allowance accordingly. Let him remember,

also, that English for speaking and English for reading are almost like two different languages; and that sermons which preach well, generally read ill. Remember these two things, I say, and I do believe you will find very much to admire in some of Whitefield's sermons. For myself, I can only say, I believe I have learned much from them, and, however great a heresy against taste it may appear, I should be ungrateful if I did not praise them.

And now let me try to point out to you what seem to me to have been the characteristic features of Whitefield's sermons. I may be wrong, but they appear to me to present just such a combination of excellencies as is most likely to make an effective preacher.

First and foremost you must remember, Whitefield preached *a singularly pure gospel*. Few men ever gave their hearers so much wheat and so little chaff. He did not get into his pulpit to talk about his party, his cause, his, interest, or his office. He was perpetually telling you about your sins, your heart, and Jesus Christ, in the way that the Bible speaks of them. "Oh, the righteousness of Jesus Christ!" he would frequently say, "I must be excused if I mention it in almost all my sermons." This, you may be sure, is the corner-stone of all preaching that God honours. It must be pre-eminently a *manifestation of truth*.

For another thing, Whitefield's preaching was *singularly lucid and simple.* You might not like his doctrine, perhaps. But at any rate you could not fail to understand what he meant. His style was easy, plain, and conversational. He seemed to abhor long and involved sentences. He always saw his mark, and went direct at it. He seldom or never troubled his hearers with long arguments and intricate reasonings. Simple Bible statements—pertinent anecdotes, and apt illustrations—were the more common weapons that he used. The consequence was, that his hearers always understood him. He never shot above their heads. Never did man seem to enter so thoroughly into the wisdom of Archbishop Usher's saying, "To make easy things seem hard is easy, but to make hard things easy is the office of a great preacher."

For another thing, Whitefield was a *singularly bold and direct preacher.* He never used that indefinite expression, "we," which seems so peculiar to English pulpit oratory, and which leaves a hearer's mind in a state of misty confusion as to the preacher's meaning. He met men face to face, like one who had a message from God to them—like an ambassador with tidings from heaven: "I have come here to speak to you about your soul." He never minced matters, and beat about the bush in attacking prevailing sins. His great object seemed to be to discover the spiritual diseases his hearers were most liable to, and then appeal directly to their hearts. The result was, that hundreds of his hearers used always to think that the sermons were specially addressed to themselves. He was not content, like many, with sticking on a tail-piece of application at the end of a long discourse. A constant vein of application ran through all his sermons. "This is for you: this is for you: and this is for you." His hearers were never let alone. Nothing, however, was more striking than his direct appeals to all classes of his congregation, as he drew towards a conclusion. With all the fault of his printed sermons, the conclusions of some of them are, to my mind, the most stirring and heart-searching addresses to souls that are to be found in the English language.

Another striking feature in Whitefield's preaching was his *tremendous earnestness*. One poor, uneducated man, said of him that he "preached like a lion." Never, perhaps, did any preacher so thoroughly succeed in showing people that he, at least, believed all he was saying, and that his whole heart, and soul, and strength, were bent on making them believe it too. No man could say that his sermons were like the morning and evening gun at Portsmouth, a formal discharge fired off, as a matter of course, that disturbs nobody. They were all life. They were all fire. There was no getting away from under them. Sleep was next to impossible. You must listen whether you liked it or not. There was a holy violence about him. Your attention was taken by storm. You were fairly carried off your legs by his energy, before you had time to consider what you would do. An American gentleman once went to hear him, for the first time, in consequence of the report he heard of his preaching powers. The day was rainy, the congregation comparatively thin, and the beginning of the sermon rather heavy. Our American friend began to say to himself, "This man is no great wonder, after all." He looked round, and saw the congregation as little interested as himself. One old man in front of the pulpit, had fallen asleep. But all at once Whitefield stopped short. His countenance changed. And then he suddenly broke forth in an altered tone: "If I had come to speak to you in my own name, you might well rest your elbows on your knees, and your heads on your hands, and sleep; and once in a while look up, and say, What is this babbler talking of? But I have not come to you in my own name. No! I have come to you in the name of the Lord of Hosts" (here he brought down his hand and foot with a force that made the building ring), "and I must, and will be heard." The congregation started. The old man woke up at once. "Ay, ay!" cried Whitefield, fixing his eyes on him, "I have waked you up, have I? I meant to do it. I am not come here to preach to stocks and stones. I have come to you in the name of the Lord God of Hosts, and I must, and will, have an audience." The hearers were stripped of their apathy at once. Every word of the sermon was attended to. And the American gentleman never forgot it.

Another striking feature in Whitefield's preaching was his *singular power of description*. The Arabians have a proverb, which says, "He is the best orator who can turn men's ears into eyes." If ever there was a speaker who succeeded in doing this, it was Whitefield. He drew such vivid pictures of the things he was dwelling upon, that his hearers could believe they actually saw them all with their own eyes, and heard them with their own ears. On one occasion," says one of his biographers, "Lord Chesterfield was among his hearers. The preacher, in describing the miserable condition of a poor benighted sinner, illustrated the subject by describing a blind beggar. The night was dark; the road dangerous, and full of snares. The poor sightless mendicant is deserted by his dog near the edge of a precipice, and has nothing to grope his way with but his staff. But Whitefield so warmed with his subject, and enforced it with such graphic power, that the whole auditory was kept in breathless silence over the movements of the poor old man;" and, at length, when the beggar was about to take that fatal step which would have hurled him down the precipice to certain destruction, Lord Chesterfield actually made a rush forward to save him, exclaiming aloud, "He is gone! he is gone!" The noble Lord had been so entirely carried away by the preacher, that he forgot the whole was a picture.

One more feature in Whitefield's preaching deserves especial notice, and that is, the immense amount of *pathos and feeling* which it always contained. It was no uncommon thing with him to weep profusely in the pulpit. Cornelius Winter goes so far as to say that he hardly ever knew him get through a sermon without tears. There seems to have been nothing whatever of affectation in this. He felt intensely for the souls before him, and his feeling found a vent in tears. Of all the ingredients of his preaching, nothing, I suspect, was so powerful as this. It awakened sympathies, and touched secret springs in men, which no amount of intellect could have moved. It melted down the prejudices which many had conceived against him. They could not hate the man who wept so much over their souls. They were often so affected as to shed floods of tears themselves. "I came to hear you," said one man, "intending to break your head, but your sermon got the better of me, it broke my heart." Once become satisfied that a man loves you, and you will listen gladly to anything he has got to say. And this was just one grand secret of Whitefield's success.

And now I will only ask you to add to this feeble sketch, that Whitefield's *action* was perfect — so perfect, that Garrick, the famous actor, gave it unqualified praise—that his *voice* was as wonderful as his action,—so powerful, that he could make thirty thousand people hear him at once—so musical and well attuned, that men said he could raise tears by his pronunciation of the word "Mesopotamia:" that his *fluency* and command of extemporaneous language were of the highest order, prompting him always to use the right word and to put it in the right place. Add, I say, these gifts to those already mentioned, and then judge for yourselves whether there is not sufficient, and more than sufficient, in our hands, to account for his power as a preacher.

For my part, I say unhesitatingly, that I believe no English preacher ever possessed such a combination of excellencies as Whitefield. Some, no doubt, have surpassed him in some of his gifts; others, perhaps, have been his equals in others. But for a combination of some of the rarest gifts which can adorn a preacher of the Gospel,—united with an unrivalled voice, delivery, action, and command of words, Whitefield, I repeat, stands alone. No man, dead or alive, I believe, ever equalled him. And, I suspect, you will always find, that just in proportion as preachers have approached that curious combination of excellencies which Whitefield possessed, just in that very proportion have they attained what Clarendon defines true eloquence to be: viz., "a strange power of making themselves believed."

5. And now, there only remains one more point connected with Whitefield to which I wish to advert. I fear that I shall have exhausted your attention already. But the point is one of such importance, that it cannot be passed over in silence. The point I mean is, *the actual amount of real good* that Whitefield did.

You will, I hope, understand me, when I say that the materials for forming an opinion on this point, in a history like his, must necessarily be scanty. He founded no denomination among whom his name was embalmed, and his every act recorded, as did John Wesley. He headed no mighty movement against a Church which openly professed false doctrines, as Luther did against Rome. He wrote no books which were to be the religious classics of the million, like John Bunyan. He was a simple, guileless man, who lived for one thing only, and that was to preach Christ. If he succeeded in doing that effectually, he cared for nothing else. He did nothing to preserve the memory of his usefulness. He left his work with the Lord.

Of course, there are many people who can see in Whitefield nothing but a fanatic and enthusiast. There is a generation that loaths everything like zeal in religion. There are never wanting men of a cautious, cold-blooded, Erasmus-like temper, who pass through the world doing no good, because they are so dreadfully afraid of doing harm. I do not expect such men to admire Whitefield, or allow he did any good. I fear, if they had lived eighteen hundred years ago, they would have had no sympathy with St. Paul.

Again, there are other people who count schism a far greater crime than either heresy or false doctrine. There is a generation of men, who, under no circumstances, will worship God out of their own parish : and as to separation from the Church, they seem to think that nothing whatever can justify it. I do not, of course, expect such men to admire Whitefield or his work. His principle evidently was, that it was far better for men to be uncanonically saved than canonically damned.

Whether by any other line of action Whitefield could have remained in the Church, and retained his usefulness is a question, which, at this distance of time, we are very incompetent to answer. That he erred in temper and judgment in his dealings with the bishops and clergy, in many instances, I have no doubt. That he raised up fresh bodies of separatists from the Church of England, and made breaches which probably will never be repaired, I have no doubt also. But still it must never be forgotten that the state of the Church was bad enough to provoke a holy indignation. The old principle is most true, that "he is the schismatic who causes the separation, and not he who separates." *If Whitefield did harm,* the harm ought to be laid on the Church which compelled him to act as he did, quite as much as on him. And when we come to strike the balance, I believe the harm he may have done is outweighed by the good a thousand-fold.

The truth I believe is, that the *direct good* Whitefield did to immortal souls was enormous. I will go further. I believe it is incalculable. In Scotland, in England, in America, creditable witnesses have recorded their testimony that he was the means of converting thousands of souls.

Franklin, the philosopher, was a cold, calculating man, and not likely to speak too highly of any minister's work. Yet even he confessed, that it "was wonderful to see the change soon made by his preaching in the manners of the inhabitants of Philadelphia. From being thoughtless or indifferent about religion, it seemed as if all the world were growing religious."

Maclaurin and Willison were Scotch ministers, whose names are well known to theological readers, and stand deservedly high. Both of them have testified that Whitefield did an amazing work in Scotland. Willison in particular says, that "God honoured him with surprising success among sinners of all ranks and persuasions."

Old Venn, in our own Church, was a man of strong common sense, as well as great grace. His opinion was, that "if the greatness, extent, success, and disinterestedness of a man's labours can give him distinction among the children of Christ, then we are warranted to affirm that scarce any one has equalled Mr. Whitefield." Again, he says, "It is a well known fact, that the conversion of men's souls have been the fruit of a single sermon from his lips, so eminently was he made a fisher of men." And, again, "Though we are allowed to sorrow that we shall never see or hear him again, we must still rejoice that millions have heard him so long, so often, and to such good effect; and that out of this mass of people, multitudes are gone before him to hail his entrance into the world of glory."

John Newton was a shrewd man, as well as an eminent minister of the Gospel. His testimony is, "I am not backward to say that I have not read or heard of any person, since the Apostles' days, of whom it may more emphatically be said, he was a burning and a shining light, than the late Mr. Whitefield, whether we consider the warmth of his zeal, the greatness of his ministerial talents, or the extensive usefulness with which the Lord honoured him."

These are not solitary testimonies. I might add many more if time permitted. Romaine did not agree with him in many things, yet what does he say of him? "We have none left to succeed him; none, of his gifts; none, of anything like him in usefulness." Toplady was a tremendously high Calvinist, and not disposed to over-estimate the number of saved souls. Yet he says, Whitefield's ministry was "attended with spiritual benefit to tens of thousands;" and he styles him "the apostle of the British empire, and the prince of preachers." Hervey was a quiet literary man, whose health seldom allowed him to quit the retirement of Weston Favell. But he says of Whitefield, "I never beheld so fair a copy of our Lord, such a living image of the Saviour. I cannot forbear applying the wise man's encomium of an illustrious woman to this eminent minister of the everlasting Gospel: 'Many sons have done virtuously, but thou excellest them all.'"

But if the amount of the direct good that Whitefield did in the world was great, who shall tell us the amount of *good that he did indirectly?* I believe it never can be reckoned up. I suspect it never will be fully known until the last day.

Whitefield was among the first *who stirred up a*

zeal for the pure Gospel among the clergy and laity of our own Church. His constant assertion of pure Reformation principles—his repeated references to the Articles, Prayer-book, and Homilies—his never answered challenges to his opponents to confute him out of the Formularies of their own communion—all this must have produced an effect, and set many thinking. I have no doubt whatever, that many a faithful minister, who became a shining light in those days within the Church of England, first lighted his candle at the lamp of a man outside.

Whitefield, again, was among the first to *show the right way to meet infidels and sceptics.* He saw clearly that the most powerful weapon against such men is not metaphysical reasoning, and critical disquisition; but preaching the whole Gospel—living the whole Gospel—and spreading the whole Gospel. It was not the writings of Leland and the younger Sherlock, and Waterland, and Leslie, that rolled back the flood of infidelity, one half so much as the preaching of Whitefield, and Wesley, and Fletcher, and Romaine, and Berridge, and Venn. Had it not been for them, I firmly believe we might have had a counterpart of the French Revolution in our own land. They were the men who were the true champions of Christianity. Infidels are seldom shaken by mere abstract reasoning. The surest arguments against them are Gospel truth, and Gospel life.

To crown all, Whitefield was the very first who seems thoroughly to have understood what Chalmers has called the *aggressive system*. He did not wait for souls to come to him, but he went after souls. He did not sit tamely by his fireside, mourning over the wickedness of the land. He went forth to beard the devil in his high places. He attacked sin and wickedness face to face, and gave them no peace. He dived into holes and corners after sinners. He hunted up ignorance and vice, wherever it could be found. He showed that he thoroughly realized the nature of the ministerial office. Like a fisherman, he did not wait for the fish to come to him. Like a fisherman, he used every kind of means. Men know a little more of this now than they did formerly. City Missions and District Visiting Societies are evidences of clearer views. But let us remember this was all comparatively new in Whitefield's time, and let us give him the credit he deserves.

In short, I come to the conclusion that no man has ever done more good in his day and generation than the man who is the subject of this lecture. He was a true hero, and that in the highest and best sense. He did a work that will stand the fire, and glorify God, when many other works are forgotten. And for that work I believe that England owes a debt to his character which England has never yet paid.

And now I hasten to a conclusion of this already over-long lecture. I have set before you, to the best of my ability, Whitefield's times, and life, and religion, and preaching, and actual work. I have not extenuated his faults, to the best of my know-ledge. I have not exaggerated his good qualities, so far as I am aware. It only remains for me to point out to you two great practical lessons which the subject appears to me to teach.

Learn then, I beseech you, for one lesson, the *amazing power that one single man possesses*, when he is determined to work for God, and has got truth on his side.

Here is a man who starts in life under many dis-advantages. He has neither family, nor place, nor money, nor high connections on his side. His views are flatly opposed to the customs and prejudices of his time. He stands in direct opposition to the stream of public taste, and the religion of the vast bulk of ministers around him. He is as much iso-lated and alone, to all appearance, as Martin Luther opposing the Pope, as Athanasius resisting the Arians, as Paul on Mars' Hill. And yet this man stands his ground. He arrests public attention. He gathers crowds around him who receive his teaching. He is made a blessing to tens of thousands. He turns the world upside down. How striking these facts are!

Here is your *encouragement*, young men, if you stand alone. You have no reason to be cast down and faint-hearted. You are not weak, though few, if God is with you. There is nothing too great to be done by a little company, if only they have Christ on their side. Away with the idea that numbers alone have power! Cast away that old vulgar error that majorities alone have strength. Get firm hold of the great truth that minorities always move the world. Think of the little flock that our Lord left behind Him, and the one hundred and twenty names in that upper chamber in Jerusalem, who went forth to assault the heathen world! Think of George Whitefield assailing boldly the ungodliness which deluged all around him, and winning victory after victory! Think of all this. Cast fear away. Lay out your talents heartily and confidently for God.

Here also is your *example*, young men, if you desire to do good to souls. Whether you become ministers, or missionaries, or teachers—never forget you must fight with Whitefield's weapons, if you wish to have any portion of Whitefield's success. Never forget what John Wesley said was Whitefield's theology,—"Give God all the glory of whatever is good in man: set Christ as high, and man as low as possible, in the business of salvation. All merit is in the blood of Christ, and all power is from the Spirit of Christ."

Think not for a moment that earnestness alone will ensure success. This is a huge delusion. It will do nothing of the kind. All the earnestness in the world will never enable a teacher of *German theology* to show you one Tinnevelly, or a teacher of *semi-Popery* one Sierra Leone. Oh, no! it must be the simple, pure, unadulterated Gospel that you must carry with you, if you are to do good. You must sow as Whitefield sowed, or you will never reap as he reaped.

Learn, in the last place, *what abundant reasons we have for thankfulness in the present condition of the Church of England.*

We are far too apt to look at the gloomy side of things around us, and at that only. We are all prone to dwell on the faults of our condition, and to forget to bless God for our mercies. There are many things we could wish otherwise in our beloved Church, beyond all question. There are defects we could wish to see remedied, and wounds we should gladly see healed. But still, let us look behind us, and compare the Church of our day with the Church of Whitefield's times. Look on this picture, and on t' / nd I am sure, if you do so honestly and fairly, ill agree with me that we have reason to be kful.

We have *bishops* on the bench now, who love the simple truth as it is in Jesus, and are ready to help

forward good works,—bishops who are not ashamed
to come forward in Exeter Hall, and lend their aid
to the extension of Christ's Gospel,—bishops who
would have welcomed a man like Whitefield, and
found full occupation for his marvellous gifts. Let
us thank God for this. It was not so a hundred
years ago.

We have hundreds of *clergymen* in our parishes
now, who preach as full a Gospel as Whitefield did,
though they may not do it with the same power,—
clergymen who are not ashamed of the doctrine of
regeneration, and do not pronounce a minister a
heretic, because he says to ungodly people, "Ye
must be born again." Let us thank God for this.
A man need not travel many miles now, in order to
find parishes where the Gospel is preached. When
driven out of one parish church, he can find truth
in another. It was not so a hundred years ago.

We have thousands of *laymen* now, who are fully
alive to the duties and responsibilities of members
of a Protestant Church,—laymen who rejoice in
holding up the hands of Evangelical ministers, and
are righteously jealous for the maintenance and extension of Evangelical truth. Let us thank God for
this. It was not so a hundred years ago.

We have *societies and agencies* for evangelizing
every dark corner of the earth in connection with
our Church. We have wide and effectual doors of

usefulness for all who are willing to labour in the Lord's vineyard. The difficulty now is, not so much to find openings for doing good, as to find men. Let us thank God for this. It was not so a hundred years ago.

Young men of the Church of England, I ask you to gather up these facts, and treasure them in your memories. They are facts. They cannot be gainsayed. Treasure them up, I repeat. Look back a century, and then look around you, and then judge for yourselves whether you ought not to be thankful.

Beware, I beseech you, of that tribe of men who would fain persuade you to forsake the Church of England, and separate from her communion. There is a generation of murmurers and complainers in the present day, who seem to revel in discovering motes in their neighbour's eyes,—a generation that seems to forget that fault-finding is the easiest task in all the world,—a generation that cannot discern the healthy parts in our body ecclesiastic, but has a wonderfully quick and morbid scent for detecting its sores,—a generation that is mighty to scatter, but impotent to build,—a generation that would persuade Churchmen to strain at gnats, but finds no difficulty itself in swallowing camels,—a generation that would have you pull the old house down, but cannot offer you so much as a tent in its place : of all such men, I say solemnly and affectionately,—of all such men,

I warn you to beware. Listen not to them. Have no friendship with them. Avoid them. Turn from them. Pass away.

Let us not leave the good old ship, the CHURCH OF ENGLAND, until we have some better reason than can at present be seen. What, though she be old and weather-beaten! What, though in some respects, she may want repair! What, though some of the crew are not to be depended on! Still, with all her faults, the old ship is in far better trim than she was a century ago. Let us acknowledge her faults, and hope they may yet be amended. But still, with all her faults, let us stick by the ship!

When the Thirty-Nine Articles of the Church of England are repealed, and the Prayer-book and Homilies so altered as to be unprotestantized,—when regeneration and justification by faith are forbidden to be preached in her pulpits,—when the Queen, Lords, and Commons, and laity, have assented to these changes,—in short, when the Gospel is driven out of the Establishment,—then, and not till then, it will be time for you and me to go out; but, till then, I say, LET US STICK TO THE CHURCH!